Quod scriptura, non iubet vetat

The Latin translates, "What is not commanded in scripture, is forbidden:'

On the Cover: Baptists rejoice to hold in common with other evangelicals the main principles of the orthodox Christian faith. However, there are points of difference and these differences are significant. In fact, because these differences arise out of God's revealed will, they are of vital importance. Hence, the barriers of separation between Baptists and others can hardly be considered a trifling matter. To suppose that Baptists are kept apart solely by their views on Baptism or the Lord's Supper is a regrettable misunderstanding. Baptists hold views which distinguish them from Catholics, Congregationalists, Episcopalians, Lutherans, Methodists, Pentecostals, and Presbyterians, and the differences are so great as not only to justify, but to demand, the separate denominational existence of Baptists. Some people think Baptists ought not teach and emphasize their differences but as E.J. Forrester stated in 1893, "Any denomination that has views which justify its separate existence, is bound to promulgate those views. If those views are of sufficient importance to justify a separate existence, they are important enough to create a duty for their promulgation ... the very same reasons which justify the separate existence of any denomination make it the duty of that denomination to teach the distinctive doctrines upon which its separate existence rests." If Baptists have a right to a separate denominational life, it is their duty to propagate their distinctive principles, without which their separate life cannot be justified or maintained.

Many among today's professing Baptists have an agenda to revise the Baptist distinctives and redefine what it means to be a Baptist. Others don't understand why it even matters. The books being reproduced in the *Baptist Distinctives Series* are republished in order that Baptists from the past may state, explain and defend the primary Baptist distinctives as they understood them. It is hoped that this Series will provide a more thorough historical perspective on what it means to be distinctively Baptist.

The Lord Jesus Christ asked, *"And why call ye me, Lord, Lord, and do not the things which I say?"* (Luke 6:46). The immediate context surrounding this question explains what it means to be a true disciple of Christ. Addressing the same issue, Christ's question is meant to show that a confession of discipleship to the Lord Jesus Christ is inconsistent and untrue if it is not accompanied with a corresponding submission to His authoritative commands. Christ's question teaches us that a true recognition of His authority as Lord inevitably includes a submission to the authority of His Word. Hence, with this question Christ has made it forever impossible to separate His authority as King from the authority of His Word. These two principles—the authority of Christ as King and the authority of His Word—are the two most fundamental Baptist distinctives. The first gives rise to the second and out of these two all the other Baptist distinctives emanate. As F.M. Iams wrote in 1894, "Loyalty to Christ as King, manifesting itself in a constant and unswerving obedience to His will as revealed in His written Word, is the real source of all the Baptist distinctives:' In the search for the *primary* Baptist distinctive many have settled on the Lordship of Christ as the most basic distinctive. Strangely, in doing this, some have attempted to separate Christ's Lordship from the authority of Scripture, as if you could embrace Christ's authority without submitting to what He commanded. However, while Christ's Lordship and Kingly authority can be isolated and considered essentially for discussion's sake, we see from Christ's own words in Luke 6:46 that His Lordship is really inseparable from His Word and, with regard to real Christian discipleship, there can be no practical submission to the one without a practical submission to the other.

In the symbol above the Kingly Crown and the Open Bible represent the inseparable truths of Christ's Kingly and Biblical authority. The Crown and Bible graphics are supplemented by three Bible verses (Ecclesiastes 8:4, Matthew 28:18-20, and Luke 6:46) that reiterate and reinforce the inextricable connection between the authority of Christ as King and the authority of His Word. The truths symbolized by these components are further emphasized by the Latin quotation - *quod scriptura, non iubet vetat*— i.e., "What is not commanded in scripture, is forbidden:' This Latin quote has been considered historically as a summary statement of the regulative principle of Scripture. Together these various symbolic components converge to exhibit the two most foundational Baptist Distinctives out of which all the other Baptist Distinctives arise. Consequently, we have chosen this composite symbol as a logo to represent the primary truths set forth in the *Baptist Distinctives Series*.

The Church
and
The Kingdom

JESSE B. THOMAS
(1832-1915)

The Church
and
The Kingdom
A New Testament Study

BY
JESSE B. THOMAS, D.D., LL.D.

*Professor Newton Theological Institution; Author
"The Old Bible and the New Science," "The Mould
of Doctrine," "Significance of the Historical
Element in Scripture," etc.*

With a Biographical Sketch of the Author by John Franklin Jones

LOUISVILLE
Baptist Book Concern
1914

The Baptist Standard Bearer, Inc.
NUMBER ONE IRON OAKS DRIVE • PARIS, ARKANSAS 72855

Thou hast given a *standard* to them that fear thee;
that it may be displayed because of the truth.
-- Psalm 60:4

Reprinted 2006

by

THE BAPTIST STANDARD BEARER, INC.
No. 1 Iron Oaks Drive
Paris, Arkansas 72855
(479) 963-3831

THE WALDENSIAN EMBLEM
lux lucet in tenebris
"The Light Shineth in the Darkness"

ISBN# 1579785212

PREFACE

The following pages embody the substance of an elective course lately given to students of Newton Theological Institution.

Some portions of the discussion (in Parts IV., V. and VI.) had been previously published in the *Western Recorder,* of Louisville, Ky. I am indebted to the courtesy of the late editor of that paper, Dr. Eaton, for permission to use the matter taken from his columns. The articles then published aroused enough interest in Wales to induce an application from the Rev. J. Spinther James, of Llandudno, for the privilege of translating them into Welsh for circulation there.

Care has been taken to derive authentic information as to the tenets of the various bodies mentioned, from the language of their official standards, supplemented by interpretative utterances of recognized leaders among them. Only representative bodies have been selected, in order to avoid needless prolixity. The effort to classify these bodies, and especially to summarize their views, is,

PREFACE

of course, a precarious one; the result must be taken "with a grain of salt." The *"logical* sequences" specified are by no means to be interpreted as *actual,* except where definitely alleged to be so. Endless differences in interpretation and application of the language of the documents cited from, are discoverable (and will probably disclose themselves in heated protest, if this volume should arrest the attention of dissidents). Moreover, logic and practice do not always travel together. Horace Walpole said the Anglican Church had "a Romish ritual, a Calvinistic creed and an Arminian clergy," and his sarcastic arrow went near the mark.

It should be added that nothing here said as to the fictitious conception of a "church universal" should be construed as questioning the substantial reality of that underlying unity of the followers of Christ throughout the ages and the world which, however wrongly named, is unquestionable. The "kingdom" is a present fact; but, thus far, only a fact "within."

Nor is there any disposition to carp at or hinder the sanguine endeavor of sincere men, clerical or lay, to hasten the visibility of Christian union by legitimate means. Doubt

PREFACE

is expressed as to supreme reliance on "business methods" of human device, or military organization into mass movements. There is peril in relying solely on the momentum of a burst of enthusiasm. The methods of the Crusades did not prove effective in the end. The kingdom of heaven is not to be "taken by violence." It will come, "not by might, nor by power, but by my Spirit, saith the Lord." It is like a "grain of mustard seed"—not a keg of dynamite.

It is not necessary to say—what will be only too obvious to the reader—that the author is a Baptist, and must be understood as speaking only from his personal point of view—not as a "master in Israel." He asks for patient reading only; not for credence, except where buttressed by the "law and the testimony."

CONTENTS

PART I. THE STUDY OF ECCLESIOLOGY.

         PAGE

I. Scope and Importance of the Study............ 11
II. Its Place in the Scheme of Christian Doctrine. 14
III. Current Problems Indirectly Involved.......... 22

PART II. MODERN NOTIONS OF THE CHURCH.

Summary of Various Uses of the Term............. 43

PART III. FORMAL DEFINITIONS.

I. The Imperial Theory.......................... 51
II. The Collegiate Theory........................ 65
III. The Sacramental Theory....................... 76
IV. The Hereditary Theory........................ 96
V. The Voluntary Theory........................ 123

PART IV. THE "HOLY CATHOLIC CHURCH."

I. The Apostles' Creed as a Basis of Unity........ 147
II. Historic Emergence of the Modern Idea of a World-church 165
III. Appeal to the New Testament in Defense of the Idea 167

CONTENTS

PART V. THE CHURCH OF THE NEW TESTAMENT.

 |PAGE
---|---

I. The Word "Ecclesia" in the New Testament... 199
II. The Greek "Ecclesia".......................... 210
III. New Testament Use of "Ecclesia" and "Basileia" 220

PART VI. CONTEMPORARY SIGNIFICANCE.

I. Importance of Distinction Urged............... 289
II. Bearing on Some Tendencies of the Present Time 296
III. Practical Conclusions 310

PART I.
THE STUDY OF ECCLESIOLOGY

I.

SCOPE AND IMPORTANCE OF THE STUDY

1. DEFINITION OF THEME.—The term "ecclesiology" has been broadened in common usage to include the detailed functions and relations of the church, as well as its essential nature. It was natural, and perhaps legitimate, that the ideal should be thus supplemented and interpreted by its actual working outcome, in order to its better understanding and appreciation. It seems, indeed, impossible to define the church without determining the range of its constituency; which involves, at once, an inquiry into the nature and significance of the ordinances. Equally preliminary to the outlining of its polity is some settlement of the nature and function of the clerical office. In these and other like particulars the subject ramifies and interlocks itself with practical problems that can not be wisely dismissed without careful investigation. The topic of ecclesiology has, accordingly, been thought worthy, in some

institutions, of being erected into a distinct department of study. It has in some instances been made to share in or absorb the realm of pastoral theology, and even of homiletics. This broader aspect of the theme will not be here wholly overlooked.

Technically speaking, however, the term "ecclesiology" points more exclusively to an inquiry into the essential nature of the church itself—into what it is, rather than what it does. The discussion thereupon takes on a theoretic rather than an experimental form, and falls legitimately within the sphere of Christian doctrine, or dogmatic theology. Especial emphasis will here be laid, therefore, upon the question of the normal constitution of the true Christian church, as defined in the New Testament, or fairly implied from its teachings.

II. Importance of the Study.—No one can read the New Testament thoughtfully without being impressed with the conspicuousness of the place there assigned to the church as a potent factor in the working out of the problems of the new era. As illustrative of the high prerogatives there assigned it, note

1. That the idea itself is of divine con-

THE STUDY OF ECCLESIOLOGY

ception, to be wrought into actuality under divine guidance and made divinely indestructible. "I will build my church" (Matt. 16: 18).

2. That it is unspeakably precious as an institution on which Christ has set his heart, and which he has "purchased with his own blood" (Eph. 5: 25; Acts 20: 28).

3. That he has chosen it to prolong and consummate his incarnate ministry. It is "his body, the fulness of him that filleth all in all" (Eph. 1: 22, 23; Col. 1: 18, 24).

4. That it is intended to become the medium of a higher revelation. Through it the "manifold wisdom of God," which "for ages has been hid," is to be "made known" (Eph. 3: 9-11).

5. That it is to be a prime instrument of personal development through its adaptation to mutual edification (Rom. 14: 19; 1 Thess. 5: 11).

6. That pecular perils and responsibilities attend its leadership, requiring high mental and spiritual qualifications and acute vigilance because of the momentousness of the interests involved (Acts 20: 28; 2 Tim. 4: 1, 2).

II.

ITS PLACE IN THE SCHEME OF CHRISTIAN DOCTRINE

I. LOGICAL ORDER.—In the development of Christian doctrine there is perceptible a natural order, in which each step seems an essential precondition to the arrival of its successor. It is well to note the place which ecclesiology normally takes in this advancing series. The theologian ordinarily treats the topics to be discussed, in the following order; viz., theology, anthropology, Christology, soteriology, ecclesiology, eschatology. It is interesting to observe also that the chronological order in which these topics actually emerged into prominence in history was almost exactly correspondent. First came the discussion of the doctrine of the Trinity, or theology proper, at the Council of Nicea in the fourth century. Next, the inquiry as to the constitution of the person of Christ, which involved anthropology as well as Christology, at the Council of Chalcedon in

THE STUDY OF ECCLESIOLOGY

the fifth century. Later, with Anselm in the twelfth century, the effort to formulate a theory of atonement brought the topic of soteriology to the front. Not until the seventeenth century, and the breaking asunder of Christendom in the Reformation under Luther, did the question of ecclesiology reach its radical form. For it became necessary then to determine whether it was essential to the true idea of the church that it should be a visible imperial organism, loss of membership in which entailed separation from Christ and salvation. The question of eschatology is still *in nubibus* in our own day. The Book of Revelation still needs most of all to be revealed. It is still the subject of the most diverse interpretations. It is last in Scripture, and remains last in yielding a definitely formulated doctrine.

Recapitulating the order of topics thus disclosed, observe

1. *The primary position of theology.* "In the beginning God;" so runs the first verse of Scripture. For without God there is no beginning of the universe, nor of intelligent thought concerning it. Science and philosophy are daily recognizing more distinctly that they can find no starting-point except

THE CHURCH AND THE KINGDOM

from this postulate. Without it cosmos returns to chaos and becomes unintelligible.

This idea is also germinal. All Scripture and all history lie hid in it. Progress must be from a beginning, and ordered progress implies guidance and purpose. So the universe comes to have a meaning, and revelation issues in prophecy. To interpret either wisely, we must "look to the end of things that are to be abolished" and "judge nothing before the time." Here, again, science and philosophy are fast falling into line with the theological implications of Scripture. The scientific theory of evolution is more and more a theory of what Henry Drummond called "Advolution." The question of origin is overshadowed by that of destiny. The unsatisfied eye turns from the *terminus a quo* to study the more significant *terminus ad quem*. (Cf. Lloyd Morgan's "Interpretation of Nature" and Thomson's "Bible of Nature"—Bross Lectures for 1907.)

On the other hand, the marked growth of so-called "Humanism" and "Personal Idealism" in philosophy reveals a disposition to turn to human personality, rather than to automatic mechanism in nature, for an explanation of the world's ongoing. Will, as

THE STUDY OF ECCLESIOLOGY

a source of energy and intelligent design (Aristotle's "Final Cause"), thus returns to a place of supremacy from which materialism would exclude it. (Cf. Lord Bacon on results of deeper study of nature.) So God becomes "first, last and midst"; for "of him and through him and to him are all things."

2. *Christology a riper manifestation of God.* Assaults on Scripture have been especially directed against the Book of Genesis and the Gospel of John—and wittingly; for in these are emphasized the beginning, in creation, and the new beginning, in the incarnation. To rob the record of either is to destroy the fruit in the seed. "In the beginning was the Logos;" but the manifestation of God was only dimly given in creation and Old Testament history. The works of creation reveal *theiotes* only, rather than *theotes* (attributes, instead of personality), as Paul tells us in his letter to the Romans (1:20). In Jesus, for the first time, the "Word became flesh," and so completely articulate. In him, for the first time, men saw the "very image of his [God's] substance" (Heb. 1:3). In his "face" shone visibly "the light of the knowledge of the glory of God" (2 Cor. 4:6). So that he might justly

say, "He that hath seen me hath seen the Father" (John 14:9), and John might say of him, "This *is* the true God, and eternal life" (1 John 5:20).

But Jesus was not only, in a unique sense, the "Son of God," being "God manifest in the flesh"; he was also the "Son of man"—the revealer of humanity, in its divine ideal and its actual condition. For, in his sinless character, he demonstrated that sin is not an originally inherent necessity of our nature—he so "condemned sin in the flesh"; and in his sorrowful experiences and tender ministries he made it clear that man has somehow "fallen short of the glory of God" destined for him. He showed also how completely the world is now "out of joint," in that his very goodness entailed the greater suffering. He revealed the true misery of man as an alien in his Father's world: "God's first-born Son—first-born in grandeur and in grief." As the typical man, he had not, like foxes or birds, a "place where to lay his head"; for man must be reminded that because he is neither fox nor bird he must be restless until he rests in God. The swine are content with husks; but the prodigal, although among swine, is not of them; and the very shame

THE STUDY OF ECCLESIOLOGY

entailed by his hunger for beasts' food compels him to remember that he is a son, and so, having come to himself, to come also to his father.

Christology thus advances beyond theology proper in that the inarticulate utterances of the earlier revelation now gather themselves into an intelligible and final word; and in that word it is made clear that God's thoughts toward man are "thoughts of peace and not of evil" (Jer. 29: 11). For Christ is "the Word" of God and Christ is incarnate love.

But Christ is the incarnation of humanity as well as of Deity. He took our nature upon him that we might become "partakers of the divine nature." He thus reveals man to himself as well as God to man. Through him we learn what man was, what he might have become, what he has become, and what he may become through grace.

3. *Soteriology the purpose of incarnation.* Bible history is the history of redemption. Creation leads providentially to re-creation. The union of God and man, in the person of Christ, is in order to the reunion of God and man in the world. Reconciliation implies prior redemption; redemption

rests upon the offering of the consummate sacrifice "once for all at the end of the ages"; and that sacrifice could come only through incarnation. Thus the "eternal purpose," that "runs through the ages," fulfilled itself in the atoning work of Christ; in which the age-long mystery of the universe is solved and "all things" are "reconciled." Only in "the fulness of time," and in its normal order, could this solution come, and only "in the fulness of time" could the notion of atonement emerge into distinct recognition.

4. *Ecclesiology the complement of soteriology.* Luke, in the Acts, speaks of those who are "being saved" (2:47). For salvation, as the Greek word etymologically implies, is bringing to completeness This involves the idea of a process. Salvation is, as Paul indicates in Phil. 2:12, a thing to be "wrought out" from incipient immaturity to ripened fullness. Regeneration is the outcome of redemption, accepted by faith, and is complete in itself. But it is the completeness of the new-born babe, who is still to develop into "a full-grown man, to the measure of the stature of the fulness of Christ." (Cf. *Teleioi kai olokleroi*"—Jas. 1:4).

It is at this point that the church emerges

THE STUDY OF ECCLESIOLOGY

into prominence as the channel in and through which the Christian life is to find its expression in the individual and the community. We thus come in due order upon the subject of our study.

The earthly church, through help of which such development is to be effected, becomes a type of, and prelude to, the arrival of that "general assembly and church of the firstborn who are enrolled in heaven" (Heb. 12:23), of which latter assembly eschatology treats, and which need here be only mentioned as the concluding feature of history, revelation, and doctrinal study, alike.

III.

CURRENT PROBLEMS INDIRECTLY INVOLVED

Certain doubts have become current in many quarters as to the true interpretation of the New Testament allusions to the then coming Church. It is not intended here to discuss the problems suggested, much less to dogmatize concerning them. They ought, however, to receive a passing notice as indicating the wide range of suggestion bred by the topic in hand, and the need of careful and patient study of the theme as essential to a confident solution of them. Among the more radical of the problems thus pressed upon thinking men is the question:

1. *Whether there is any warrant for the existence of the organized Church, or any need for its persistence.*

(1) Radical criticism denies the trustworthiness of the Gospel records, and consequently makes it impossible to ascertain what words Christ actually used. At the

THE STUDY OF ECCLESIOLOGY

best he is represented as having employed the critical word *ecclesia* but twice, and that by only one of the Evangelists. And only one of these allusions is confidently relied on as genuine in so influential a work as Thayer's "Dictionary of New Testament Greek." Moreover, if he spoke Aramaic only, he could not have used the identical word in question, but only one reckoned by the reporter as its equivalent. In the only unquestioned case (Matt. 18: 17) the allusion seems to be an existing institution, probably the synagogue. What evidence, then, remains that Christ ever expected or intended the arising of such an institution?

(2) Even supposing it certain that he employed the word in question, or its equivalent, there remains still the doubt whether he had in mind or purpose a formally organized body. The institutionalism of his time was frowned upon by him. He foreshadowed a new era in which emphasis would attach to that which is "within"—a "worship in spirit," as contrasted with the sensuous externalism of Judaism. "Institutional Christianity" has accordingly been bitterly denounced as a perverse misrepresentation of Christ's fundamental idea. Pleas

THE CHURCH AND THE KINGDOM

have been made for a "creedless, formless, nameless Christianity." The Young Men's Christian Associations have been denounced as "exponents of an effete theology and recruiting clubs for the old churches" because they do not swing out upon the broad sea of so-called "Liberalism," and, ignoring the Church wholly, "work for ends that are purely moral and spiritual and Christian." A prominent minister in one of our large cities is reported as saying: "I don't believe Christ ever intended to found a Church in the modern sense of that term. . . . Jesus Christ came to establish God's kingdom on earth." And this from an "orthodox" pulpit.

(3) Moreover, supposing the formal Church to have been a normal development in the beginning, there is room for doubt as to its permanent usefulness. Having been born of Judaism, and having taken on a Judaistic tinge, may it not have outgrown its earlier conditions? May it not now need to be put aside like other "childish" things inherited from "them of old time"? Roman Catholicism may have been a judiciously devised cocoon for a crude populace, but ought not such swaddling-clothes to be recognized as outgrown? Ralph Waldo Emer-

THE STUDY OF ECCLESIOLOGY

son abandoned the ministry rather than share in the administration of a purely "carnal" ordinance—the Lord's Supper—alleging that it was "against his constitution." One writer remarks that "the theory seems to be gaining ground among advanced thinkers that just in the degree that the Kingdom of heaven gets itself established on earth, through the Church, perhaps, as chief agency, will the Church itself become a superfluity; and the ethical societies of America and Europe are already discussing the question, 'To what good purpose shall we devote church edifices when the organizations that erected them, and used them one day out of seven for religious observances, shall have yielded place to organizations and methods better adapted to advance the intellectual and moral interests of the human family?'"

2. *Questions have arisen as to the normal constituency of a Christian church.*

(1) Must it, in order to merit the name lawfully, be composed exclusively of those who have voluntarily attached themselves to it? In some countries every citizen is, by virtue of his citizenship, constituted a member. In some communions birth into a

Christian household carries the babe into membership. It is contended in some quarters that the "world," as a "subject of redemption," is itself a Church. And, again, baptism by an authorized hand is supposed to "christen," thus incorporating the baptized into the Church.

(2) What of the requirement of definite belief in Christ, or salvation through his intervention in any form? The "Broad Church," the "liberals," the "ethical reformers," sharply assail credalism as obstructive, if not destructive, in tendency. Formulas of all kinds, it is said, have arrested development, bred tyranny, and ended in persecution. "He can't be wrong whose life is in the right." "Out of the heart," not out of the head, are "the issues of life." The Presbyterian Church requires subscription to a creed only of the ordained. Anglicans rebel against such subscription as "a yoke that neither we nor our fathers could bear." But why should any informal profession of faith be required, since sincerely good intent, wholly apart from intellectual attitude, is alone essential?

(3) Is there need of any prior experience of inward change—any hint of what is

THE STUDY OF ECCLESIOLOGY

known as regeneration—to be insisted on? Is regeneration to be regarded as a condition, or, at best, an inseparable sequence, if not a product, of baptism? The followers of Alexander Campbell have long been estranged from their baptismal coreligionists because of the impression, whether truly or falsely derived from their utterances, that they regard baptism as strictly "christening" its recipient, apart from any anterior experience other than intellectual and voluntary. It is plausibly urged by them that acceptance of Christ as Teacher and King may be definitely shown in submission to his command. All avowal of emotional change is unverifiable and apt to be delusive. Whatever may have been his occult experiences, therefore, he becomes overtly a "Christian" only through the appointed channel of outward expression of discipleship.

(4) Is baptism, as an outward act, essential to legitimate membership in a normally constituted church? The Friends, for instance, a most devout and gracious people, wholly repudiate all obligation to observe ordinances in literal form. The disposition to remand varying forms of baptism to non-essentialism, as touching an "externality

of an externality," has much increased in later days. The hunger for ecclesiastical unity tends to benumb and stifle any too curious inquiry into the cogency of traditional scruples as to departure from exact obedience. Why should the "seamless coat" of Christ be rent through obstinate clinging to divisive externalisms? In some churches resort has been had to "affiliated membership." In England "mixed" churches, often having pastors of variant faith, abound. It is not unusual to invite to the Lord's table all those who count themselves Christians, without regard to open profession of faith and baptism, or alliance with any church.

3. *Serious questioning of the wisdom of prolonging of denominational distinctions begins to become insistent.* The alleged weakness of divided Protestantism over against the compactness of the Church of Rome, the growth of social and national tendencies toward unification in organization, and especially the expressed desire of our Lord for the oneness of his followers, have awakened renewed doubts as to the legitimacy of the partition lines that now isolate Christendom into sects. Such questions as these are becoming rife; viz.:

THE STUDY OF ECCLESIOLOGY

(1) Was the original breaking up of Protestantism into Lutheran and Reformed bodies needful or wise? It is remarked that the tendency so initiated has gone on with increasing intensity until resultant bodies have grown "thick as leaves in Vallombrosa." As a result, there have followed friction, individual weakening, fossilization, and unfavorable impression on the outward world. "I have lived too long in a country where people worship cows," said Lord Macaulay, "to think much of the differences that part Christians from Christians." Pres. A. D. White, in 1875, denounced the intrusion of denominationalism into education. He insisted that it had created "only a multitude of little sectarian schools with pompous name and poor equipment, each doing its best to prevent the establishment of any institution broader and better."

On the other hand, Dr. Philip Schaff, a most competent authority, vigorously defended the existing order. "Denominations," he asserted, "are most numerous in the most advanced and active sections of the world. A stagnant church is a sterile mother. . . . Sects are a sign of life and interest in religion. The most important periods of the Church—the Nicene age and the age of the Reformation—were full of controversy."

An earnest plea for the revival of **denominational** enthusiasm was also later issued by an influential Presbyterian paper. It claimed that "diffusive Christianity is no more effective in saving men than sheet-lightning shimmering over summer clouds." The editor thinks that all the Christianity in the world has been almost entirely the product of denominational zeal and enterprise. He feels assured that Christian work, to be greatly and permanently **effective**, should be divided up, carried on and sustained by denominations, and in furtherance of this view continues:

"Denominationalism, intense, intelligent and loyal, forcing itself into power by saving men, is not a curse, but a blessing. If the world is saved, it will be saved in this way. Undenominational efforts, however well meant, and however apparently successful, have always failed of permanent results, and as long as human nature exists as it is, always will fail. Denominationalism is not what is popularly called sectarianism; it does not promote bigotry. The most

THE STUDY OF ECCLESIOLOGY

abominable dogmatism extant is among those who boast that they have no creeds. It is a sort of headless monster, flopping itself about without law of existence, unregulated by the equities of truth or charity."

(2) But, admitting that some lines of partition are advisable, and even inevitable, it remains to inquire at what point such partition becomes needful or advisable. Most denominations divide upon details of polity, upon creedal differences, or upon questions of ritual or outward detail. Baptists and Episcopalians are ordinarily singled out by a common instinct as chief obstructionists of the final reunion of Christendom. For it is seen that the points at which they dissent from other bodies are most radical. For Baptists pertinaciously adhere to immersion as the only authorized baptism, and therefore essential to the normal constituency of a New Testament church. While the Episcopalians, with equal fidelity, claim that ordination at the hands of the "historic episcopate" is essential to clerical efficiency, and therefore to legitimate baptism itself. Questions of polity or ritual are largely questions of expediency; but questions of supposed fidelity to express command or

to divinely established order are not so.

4. *New social, political and other conditions are pressing anew upon us the inquiry as to the nature and range of the functions of the Church.*

(1) Ought the Church any longer to attempt the supervision of private conduct by way of discipline; and, if so, for what? The English Church agrees with Augustine that the parable of the "tares" forbids any interference with the growing crop; to root out offenders is to interfere with the work of the angels. Let all "grow together until the harvest." Although Charles Darwin was a professed agnostic up to his death, there was no hesitation in reading the burial service over him as having died in the "odor of sanctity." Trials for heresy have come to engender bitterer criticism of the heresy-hunter than of the heretic. He who boldly departs from and sneers at the common faith is no longer a "miscreant." He is more likely to be crowned, by the secular press at least, as a hero. "Worldly amusements" were once thought to be deserving of ecclesiastical notice, and those who shared in them were subjected to the humiliation of being "labored with," and, if obstinate, of

THE STUDY OF ECCLESIOLOGY

being cut off. But matters of personal behavior are no longer the subject of espionage or adjudication in the Church—save in the case of criminal or other outrageous offense. What such relaxation of traditional "watch-care" may ultimately bring forth, is not yet clear.

(2) Pre-eminent a m o n g the growing problems of the day, perhaps the one supreme subject of hesitating inquiry is that of the relation of the Church, as such, to economic and other social questions. What attitude ought the Church to assume toward labor organizations, and toward the whole movement which they, in part, represent? What of the work of "institutional churches," and official participation in efforts for social betterment among the poor and the vicious? How far may the Church properly go in seeking municipal or other corporate advance in such betterment? At what point ought the Church to stop in the effort to combine the ethical and the strictly religious? Is there any danger of swamping the latter in the former? It is needless to particularize further. The intricacies of the problem are labyrinthine.

Dean Fremantle, in his book on "The

THE CHURCH AND THE KINGDOM

World as a Subject of Redemption," sharply repels the common notion that the mission of the Church is primarily to the individual. He there says: "Salvation is looked upon mainly as the deliverance of individuals. The idea of salvation of society has been ignored, though it stands out prominently in both the Old Testament and the New Testament. . . . The main object of Christian effort is not to be found in either the saving individuals out of a ruined world, or in the organizing of a separate society destined always to hold aloof from the world, but in saving the world itself" (pp. 7, 9).

Dr. R. J. Campbell, the brilliant successor of Joseph Parker in the City Temple, London, in his "New Theology Sermons," thus exalts the present social functions of the Church:

"As to the function of Christianity. *'Other-worldism'* has in reality nothing to do with Christianity. . . . The Church of Jesus originally knew of no commission to get men ready for a heaven beyond the tomb. . . . Co-operation must replace competition; brotherhood must replace individualism; the weakest (morally and physically) must be the objects of the tenderest care

THE STUDY OF ECCLESIOLOGY

which the community can show; selfishness must be driven out by love. This is the whole Christian programme" (Pref. IX. X.).

Not so confident or optimistic are the conclusions of a returned missionary as to the observed workings of this theory on the foreign field. As the result of long personal acquaintance with the facts, he notes that the ratio of conversions was never so small in proportion to the exertions put forth; that conversions among the heathen are not in the ratio of the difference of the means employed sixty years ago, while schoolteaching and general intelligence are greater; that respect for Christianity, through its missionaries, has increased and is increasing, but, if we contrast the results of present activities as to conversions, the difference is most perceptible. He asks why this is so, and then gives reasons as follows:

"It is not that the missionary is less industrious and self-sacrificing; he is vastly better equipped in every way for his work. The trouble is that his exertions are too general. The attempt is made to cover too much ground. Besides, there has been the counteractive influence of the popular notion that Christianity is rather for the betterment

THE CHURCH AND THE KINGDOM

of the race in its general conditions than for the saving of souls from eternal ruin.

"The churches have fallen into the channels of mere humanitarianism. The trend now is toward municipal Christianity. Christian power is diverted to reputable secularities, ethics, and enfranchisements, in order to greater political liberty, until the operation of Christian sacrifice comes in only incidentally, soul-saving being not the only, or even the main, end or object. Everybody is preaching everywhere to the masses, but who is preaching, and quietly bending all his energies, to save the individual? Where is the society for solitary auditors? Where is the house-to-house organization to wrestle with the unsaved alike in the slums and behind brownstone fronts? The name 'slums' generally shuts the door against all efforts in the more destitute portions of our cities. Work for the improvement of moral natures is spread out, like a little butter over a whole loaf."

(3) The exclusion of the Bible from the public schools, and the consequent antagonism of the Roman Catholic clergy to them as "godless"; the embarrassments connected with stringent Sunday legislation; the

THE STUDY OF ECCLESIOLOGY

scarcely concealed ambition and effort of Romish prelates to secure political predominance in the country—call for more definite conception of the duty of the Church and its ministry as to political affairs. Are we a "Christian nation," as our Supreme Court has affirmed, and, if so, has such a nation any duty to realize Christian ideals in its legislation, and what part, if any, in securing such legislation belongs to the Church?

5. *Changing social and other conditions suggest new queries as to the true status and functions of the Christian ministry.*

(1) Is the ministry intrinsically a lifelong office, and must it therefore be so continued? The motto, "Once a priest, always a priest," was inherited from the Romish Church, where even the pope could not efface the indelible seal of ordination. The notion of a clerical caste, thus engendered, was frowned upon by the early dissenters from Rome. The Independent churches, including the Baptists, ordained to a local pastorate only. That pastorate ending, his ministerial function ended with it. A new ordination must equip him for a new location. There were in those days no "reverend" coal-dealers or insurance agents, or ministers

"without charge." The sacred and secular were not, indeed, far apart; for it was not thought indecorous for the church to set over it a "consecrated cobbler" or Bunyan-like "tinker." In our day, when the average pastor receives less than half the compensation awarded to the skilled mechanic, there seems strong temptation to revert to the Pauline self-support as a final alternative.

(2) A cognate question arises in view of the multiplication of itinerant workers, evangelistic and other. May one be lawfully ordained to a special form of non-pastoral service? May we rightly "lay hands" on a brother to accredit him specifically to the work of a missionary, as they did in the case of Barnabas and Saul, when they "sent them away" to the Gentiles? May one be ordained as a colporter, a Sunday-school organizer, a Bible reader, a "settlement" worker? Lay work rapidly takes on clerical aspects; may ordination be adjusted anew to its demands?

6. *The old question of the proposed "enrichment of the service" recurs with varying local atmosphere and increasing obeisance to the demands of higher esthetic culture.* Shall we return to the rigorous observance

THE STUDY OF ECCLESIOLOGY

of the Christian Year, to surpliced choirs, to a prescribed liturgy, to the recital of the Apostles' Creed and the Ten Commandments? And can we all agree upon the same routine of service? Is there any danger that in refusing, as John Wesley did, to "let the devil have all the good tunes," we may unwittingly install the devil also as choir-master? How far may we go in subsidizing sense to the help of spirit?

Only a few of the perplexing queries that swarm out of the depths have been thus hinted at. Their intelligent solution is of the highest importance. But, in order to this, there is need of patient and thorough study of the preliminary question as to the divine ideal of the Church itself.

PART II.
MODERN NOTIONS OF THE CHURCH

I.

SUMMARY OF VARIOUS USES OF THE TERM

I. SUBORDINATE CONCEPTIONS.

1. *Colloquial.*

(1) The house of worship is familiarly known as the church. This is metaphorical only. The New Testament church was not the house, but *"in* the house."

(2) The public service is also loosely referred to, under the expression "going to church." It is needless to say that this is also purely conventional.

2. *Vaguely comprehensive.*

(1) Christianity at large is sometimes referred to; as in the antithesis between the "church" and the "world." The phrase "church history" is ordinarily understood as equivalent to the history of the Christian religion. This is a natural, but sometimes misleading, expansion of the original meaning of the term.

(2) All truly religious people are some-

times swept under the shadow of the word "church"—and this quite unwarrantably. Bishop Hurst, in his "Church History," thus writes: "The actual Church, in distinction from the Christian, includes all believers in whom the Divine Spirit dwells, apart from ecclesiastical relations. The general Church is of still broader scope. It consists of all worshipers of Jehovah in pre-Christian ages, and of persons of pure purpose in all ages, who have lived according to their light" (Vol. I., p. 15).

3. *Qualified.*

(1) Generic divisions. We thus divide the Christian world into its great segments as Greek, Roman Catholic, Protestant. Each of these is corporately known as a church.

(2) Doctrinal groupings. Protestantism is broadly divided into the Evangelical and so-called "Liberal" branches. A distinction less conspicuous now than in former days is that which disinguished the Calvinistic from the Arminian sections.

(3) National or sectional designations. All the local bodies belonging to the state church are included under the common name of the "Anglican Church." In this country

the voluntary consolidation of individual churches make up what is known as the Presbyterian Church of America. In like manner we refer to the Methodist Episcopal Church, South or North.

(4) Denominational groupings. Churches, not organically affiliated, but akin in doctrine and polity, are likewise known as Lutheran, Presbyterian, Baptist, and the like. A certain unity of relation is thus implied.

(5) Parties in a single body are sometimes discriminated by this term. Thus we speak of the Broad Church, the High Church, and other sections of the Anglican body.

II. Fundamental Distinction of Meaning.—All accidental and inferential senses of the word may, for the purposes of this inquiry, be ignored. All conceptions of the Church settle down into two, which are intrinsically distinct.

1. *The Church universal.* This conception covers a vast variety of subordinate particulars, often obscure or incongruous, as will hereafter be seen. It may be visible or invisible or both; it may be organized or diffused; it may be contemporary or inde-

terminate in temporal range, as defined in various standards.

2. *The church, l o c a l and individual.* That a local organization fashioned after the New Testament model may be properly spoken of as *a* church nobody questions, nor that churches may be thus recognized as legitimately so designated. But it is sharply questioned whether *"the* church" can ever be rightly understood as referring to such a local body, either individually or generically.

It is further often insisted that the primary meaning of the word forbids its application, except in a metaphorical sense, to the local body; the part is put for the whole.

III. CLASSIFICATION OF THEORIES.—The following theories are to be examined in order, reference being had to the formularies of the various bodies holding them as the most authoritative source of information concerning them; interpreted, occasionally, by representative men.

I. *The Imperial Theory:* A visible world empire, under a visible head.

II. *The Collegiate Theory:* A confederation of kingdoms.

III. *The Sacramental Theory:* U n i t y

MODERN NOTIONS OF THE CHURCH

through sacramental uniformity; a "communion of saints."

IV. *The Hereditary Theory:* An elect community continuous through heredity.

V. *The Voluntary Theory:* A local body entered by individual consent.

PART III.
FORMAL DEFINITIONS

I.

THE IMPERIAL THEORY

The only church consistently claiming to be visibly one and universal in character is the Papal. For a trustworthy conception of its theory of the constitution and characteristics of the Church, let us turn to the language of its documentary standards, supplemented by the utterances of its accredited theologians.

I. OFFICIAL STANDARDS.—The formal decrees of the Council of Trent give no explicit definition of the Church. But in 1565 there was issued by its authority a "Profession of the Tridentine Faith," containing the following clause from Bulls of Pius IV.:

"X. I acknowledge the Holy Catholic Apostolic Roman Church for the mother and mistress of all churches; and I promise and swear true obedience to the Bishop of Rome, successor to St. Peter, Prince of the Apostles, and Vicar of Jesus Christ" (Schaff,

"Creeds of Christendom," II., 209; McElhinney, "Doct. of Church," 186).

In the "Catechism of the Council," put forth in 1566, is a fuller statement, as follows: "The Church, according to St. Augustine's definition, is the body of the faithful dispersed throughout the world. . . . The wicked are contained in the Church as the chaff is mingled with grain on the threshing-floor, or as dead members sometimes remain attached to a living body. . . . Only three classes of persons are excluded from her pale: first, infidels; next, heretics and schismatics; and, lastly, the excommunicated. Infidels, because they never belonged to and never knew the Church, nor were ever made partakers of the sacraments in the communion of a Christian people (this includes pagans, Mohammedans and Jews). Heretics and schismatics, because they have severed themselves from the Church. They are still, however, subject to the power of the Church, seeing that they may be cited before her tribunal, punished and condemned by anathema. Finally, excommunicated persons also, because excluded by her sentence from the Church, belong not to her communion until they repent. As to the rest, although shameful and wicked persons, there is no doubt that they still continue in the Church; and of this the faithful are frequently to be informed, in order that they may have the assurance that even were the lives of her ministers debased by crime, they are still included in her pale, and forfeit, on that account, none of their prerogatives.

"The *first* distinctive character of the true Church is *unity*. . . . This Church has also one Ruler and Governor, the *invisible Christ,* whom the eternal Father hath made head over all the Church, which is his body; but *the visible* is he who, the legitimate successor of Peter, the prince of the apostles, occupies the See of Rome. . . . As a visible Church requires a visible head, our Saviour appointed Peter head and pastor of all the faithful, when, in the most ample terms, He committed to his care the feeding of his sheep, so as that He willed his successor to have the very same power of ruling and governing the whole Church. . . .

"As to the *second* distinctive mark of the Church—*holiness*. . . . The Church, although containing many sinners, is called holy . . . the faithful, though offending in many things, are called holy because they have been made the people of God, or have consecrated themselves to Christ by faith and baptism. . . . Yet, further, the Church alone has the legitimate worship of sacrifice, and the salutary use of the sacraments, by which, as by the efficacious instruments of divine grace, God effects true holiness: so that *whosoever are really holy can not be outside this Church.* . . .

"The *third* distinctive m a r k of the Church is that she is called *Catholic*—that is, universal—as embracing, in the bosom of her love, all mankind; . . . and as comprehending all the faithful who have existed from Adam up to the present day, or who shall exist to the end of time. . . . "We may *also* know the true Church from her origin, which she derives, under the revelation of grace, *from the apostles;* for her doctrines are neither novel nor of recent origin, but delivered of old by the apostles, and diffused throughout the world. . . . Wherefore, that all might know the true Catholic Church, the Fathers, guided by the Spirit of God, added in the creed the word 'apostolic.' . . . Being thus divinely guided, this one Church can not err in delivering the discipline of faith and morals; but all other societies, calling themselves churches, guided as they are by the spirit of the devil, are necessarily sunk in the most pernicious errors both of doctrine and morals" (McElhinney, *ut sup.*, 186-190).

II. INTERPRETATION AND DEFENSE OF THE THEORY BY ROMANIST WRITERS.—It will be observed that the essential feature of the above definitions is affirmance of the reality of an external and visible organism, in which apostolic leadership and authority have been continued representatively in Peter's official successors, and into which men must be incorporated by external acts alone. Thus Bellarmine says: "We do not think there is any internal virtue required, but only profession of faith and participation of the sacraments, which is recognized by sense. For the Church is an assembly of men, as visible and palpable as the company of the Roman people, or the Kingdom of France, or the Republic of Venice" (cited in Hodge, "Church Polity," 19).

Again, Moehler explains that "the ultimate reason of the visibility of the Church is to be found in the *incarnation* of the Divine Word. . . . The Deity having manifested its action in Christ according to an

THE CHURCH AND THE KINGDOM

ordinary human fashion, the form in which his work was to be continued, was thereby traced out. The preaching of his doctrine needed now a visible medium, and must be entrusted to visible envoys, teaching and instructing after the wonted method. . . . Thus, the *visible Church*, from the point of view here taken, *is the Son of God himself* among men *in a human form,* perpetually renovated and eternally young—the permanent incarnation of the same, as, in Holy Writ, even the faithful are called the 'body of Christ' " (Symbolism, N. Y., 1844, 332, 333).

Cardinal Newman, in his "Sermons on Subjects of the Day" (Sermons XIV., XV., XVI.), appeals to the prophecies of the Old Testament in support of the theory that the New Testament Church must needs be such a visible imperial power. For the promise in Isaiah (37:31) that a "remnant" of Judah should survive and prosper, taken in connection with frequent other prophetic allusions to the preservation of such a "remnant," clearly foreshadows a future organism in continuance of the Jewish—a new form of an old and imperishable thing. As confirming this "principle of continuity," he

FORMAL DEFINITIONS

turns to the apostolic rebuke of the Colossians for returning to the "rudiments of the world" in worship (Col. 2: 20-22). This return he interprets as not a revival of Jewish rites, but a substitution of heathen customs for the divinely ordained ritual given the Jews. The new Israel, he insists, should have continued priesthood, sacrifice, incense, and the like, after the only divinely given pattern. For proof that the new Israel was meant to be a "visible imperial power," like the old of which it is a modified prolongation, and not merely a "conformity to creed or philosophy," he turns to various Old Testament passages. He claims that the prediction in Isa. 2: 2, for instance, that "the mountain of the Lord's house" shall be "exalted above the hills," and become a source of attraction and authority to all people, implies a supreme earthly sovereignty. "An invisible kingdom on the earth" he declares to be inconceivable. Christ is now, indeed, an invisible ruler, but his earthly rule must be made visible. This rule was promised his apostles: "Ye shall sit upon twelve thrones" (Matt. 19: 28). And Peter was made their head as chief repository of authority (Matt. 16: 18). The parable of the mustard seed in Matthew, it is urged, refers unmistakably to the same thing as the growing *"tree"* in Dan. 4: 10-12, in which the "birds of the air" took refuge. Parallel with this is also the "cedar" in Ezek. 17: 22-24, in the "shade of whose branches" "birds of every wing shall dwell." In both these figures an overshadowing kingdom is indicated. This is still more explicitly predicted in the prophetic figures of Dan. 2: 31-45. For if the earlier kingdoms referred to be actual—viz., Rome and Persia—consistency requires that the final conquering kingdom be also earthly. But this kingdom is clearly the Church (cf. Apoc. 19, 11: 14, 15).

III. SUMMARY OF PAPAL THEORY.

1. It holds that the "Holy Catholic Church" is a visible, world-embracing organism—identical with the "kingdom of heaven" foretold by the prophets and announced by our Lord as "at hand" (cf. Newman *sup.*).

2. That Peter was by Christ himself made sole head of that kingdom; and invested, as his substitute, with all his own attributes and powers. Peter thus became a prolonged incarnation of the Divine. To doubt his official word or resist his au-

FORMAL DEFINITIONS

thority is therefore to doubt and resist God.

3. That the sovereign pontiff, as the successor of Peter, inherits all the powers and prerogatives of Peter himself; becoming thus the sole medium through whom the wisdom, power and grace of God can directly reach men.

4. That there is no forgiveness of sin, and no salvation, outside the Church; and that, within the Church, absolution of sin and bestowal of grace are obtainable only at the hands of priests, lawfully ordained by bishops empowered thereto by the supreme head of the Church.

As illustrating these conceptions, note the following Papal utterances; viz.:

Innocent III., at his inauguration in 1198, announced himself as "the vicegerent of Christ; the successor of Peter . . . less than God, more than man . . . who judges all, is judged by none."

Boniface VIII., at his coronation in 1294, declared himself "Father of princes and kings, ruler of the world, vicar on earth of Jesus Christ our Saviour."

The same pope, in the famous bull *"Unam Sanctam,"* claims that as "the spiritual power is above the temporal," "whoever resists the highest power ordained of God resists God himself."

The *Civilta Cattolica,* official organ of the Papacy, in 1871 defined the functions of the pope as follows: He is "the chief justice of the civil law. In him the two powers, the spiritual and temporal, meet together as in their head; for he is the vicar of Christ, who is not only eternal priest, but also 'King of kings and Lord of lords'" (Dollinger, "Dec'ns and Letters," etc.).

IV. LOGICAL SEQUENCES OF THEORY.

1. *As to the individual.*

(1.) Salvation is obtainable, not through faith in Jesus Christ, nor through regeneration by the Holy Spirit, but through the external rite of baptism lawfully administered. (See Bellarmine, *sup.* p. 20.)

(2) Forgiveness of sins can come only through priestly intervention. "Absolution is that act of the priest whereby in the sacrament of penance he frees men from sin . . . (requiring) on the part of the minister previous valid reception of the order of priesthood, and jurisdiction granted by competent authority over the person receiving the sacrament" (Cath. Encyc., 1907, *s. v.* "Absolution").

FORMAL DEFINITIONS

(3) Through the power of "the keys," jurisdiction over purgatory is also in the hands of the Church, and "plenary indulgence for the living and the dead" may be granted by the Pope, releasing men from the penalty of sins not yet committed, or from the pains of purgatory.

(4) "Saving faith" is reliance upon the authority of the Pope as the only infallible interpreter of Scripture, and guide in all questions of belief and conduct. The claim of the right of private interpretation of Scripture, and "liberty of conscience" in obedience thereto, was denounced by Pius IX. (citing Gregory XVI., 1832) as "insanity."

2. *As to the nation.*

(1) No civil government is lawful if heretical; that is, if not instituted or sanctioned by Papal authority.

Leo XIII., in Encyc., January, 1890, says: "In very truth Jesus Christ gave to his apostles unrestrained authority in regard to things sacred, together with the most genuine and true power of making laws, as also with the twofold right of judging and of punishing which flow from that power: 'All power is given to me in heaven and in

THE CHURCH AND THE KINGDOM

earth,' etc. . . . There is 'a certain orderly connection of church and state which may be compared to the union of soul and body.' "

(2) A government failing to extirpate heresy may be dissolved by Papal decree. The Lateran Council of 1215 ordained that if "heresy be allowed by the king to grow in his dominions, . . . the Pope may declare the vassals of that ruler absolved from his fealty and invite Catholics to occupy the country" (Addis and Emmett's Dict., s. v. "Deposing Power").

This doctrine is still avowed. "The very fact that European governments have ceased to be Christian makes it impossible for the Papacy, of which Christ and his gospel are the life, to live at peace with them. . . . The Pope must oppose, must be out of sympathy with the civil power when he sees it establishing schools without religion, encouraging the erection of heretical temples, vexing and banishing religious orders, and throwing obstacles in the way of those who wish to embrace the religious life" (Addis and Emmett, Dictionary, s. v. "States of the Church").

(3) The Pope may lawfully require the suppression of heresy by force. The argu-

FORMAL DEFINITIONS

ment of dissenters in England against the interference of the Anglican Church with freedom of worship fails as against the Roman Catholic Church, "for if the magistrate allow himself to be guided by the Church and the Pope, he rests on the basis of infallible truth, and his action in applying the forces of the establishment to the support of religion can not, in that case, be either mistaken or mischievous" (Addis and Emmett, Dictionary, *s. v.* "Establishment of Church").

The "Roman Catholic Dictionary," from which the above citations are made, was published in 1885 under the *imprimatur* of the highest Papal authority in England.

In further confirmation of the inferential conclusions above set forth may be added the following familiar utterances of one of the most revered of the popes, his *dicta* being since reinforced by Papal approval.

From the syllabus of Pius IX., put forth in 1864, and subsequently, "by the Decree of Infallibility, confirmed as truths eternal and equal in authority with the Decalogue":

"The State has not the right to leave every man free to profess and embrace whatever religion he shall deem true.

THE CHURCH AND THE KINGDOM

"It has not the right to the entire direction of public schools."

In the same syllabus, conversely, the rights and powers of the Church are thus put forth:

"She has the right to require the State not to leave every man free to profess his own religion.

"She has the right to deprive the civil authority of the entire government of the public schools.

"She has the right of perpetuating the union of Church and State.

"She has the right to require that the Catholic religion shall be the only religion of the State, to the exclusion of all others.

"She has the right to prevent the State from granting the public exercise of their own worship to persons immigrating into it.

"She has the power of requiring the State not to permit free expression of opinion."

II.

THE COLLEGIATE THEORY

Closely allied, in its dominant ideas, to the imperial theory is the collegiate. As typical illustrations of it, we may refer to the organization of the Eastern, or Greek, and the Anglican bodies. Referring to the official or otherwise authoritative utterances of these, we find the following conception of the Church outlined:

I. CREEDAL AND OTHER DEFINITIONS.

1. *Eastern or Greek Church.*—The *"Confessio Dosithei,"* one of the "Acts of the Synod of Jerusalem" (1672), reckoned by Dr. Schaff "the most authoritative and complete doctrinal deliverance of the modern Greek Church," contains the following statements; viz.:

"Art. X. The Holy Catholic and Apostolic Church comprehends all true believers in Christ, and is governed by Christ, the only head, through duly ordained bishops in *unbroken succession*. The doctrine of the

THE CHURCH AND THE KINGDOM

Calvinists, that bishops are not necessary, or that priests (presbyters) may be ordained by priests, and not by bishops only, is rejected.

"Art. XI. Members of the Christian Church are *all the faithful* who firmly hold the faith of Christ as delivered by him, *the apostles, and the holy synods,* although some of them may be subject to various sins" (Schaff, "Creeds of Christendom," I: 62-64. A condensation. The full creed in Greek and Latin is given in same work: II: 410-416).

The "Catechism of the Orthodox Eastern Church" (1839) says (in answer to Q. 252): "The Church is a divinely instituted community of men, united by the orthodox faith, the law of God, the *hierarchy,* and the *sacraments.*"

In reply to the question, "How can the Church, which is visible, be the object of faith ("I believe in the Holy Catholic Church"), when faith, as the apostle says, is the 'evidence of things not seen'?" it is answered: "First, though the Church be visible, the grace of God which dwells in her, and in those who are sanctified in her, is not so; and this it is which properly con-

FORMAL DEFINITIONS

stitutes the object of faith in the Church.

"Secondly, the Church, though visible so far as she is upon earth, and contains all orthodox Christians living upon earth, still is at the same time invisible, so far as she is also partially in heaven, and contains all those that have departed hence in true faith and holiness."

To the further question, "How does it agree with the unity of the Church that there are many separate and independent churches, as those of Jerusalem, Antioch, Alexandria, Constantinople, Russia?" the reply is that "these are particular churches, or *parts* of the *one Catholic* Church: the separateness of their visible organization does not hinder them from being all spiritually great *members* of the *one body* of the *universal Church*, from having one head, Christ; and one spirit of faith and grace. This unity is expressed outwardly by unity of creed, and by communion of prayer and *sacraments*" (McElhinney, "Doct. of Church," Ch. XVIII., pp. 196, 197).

In the catechisms (Part I., Sec. 10) occur the following utterances concerning the sacraments:

1. In the Greek Catechism, Jerusalem

Ed., page 82, we read, "It is one of the presumptuous sins against the Holy Spirit, to hope for salvation without works to merit it."

2. A sacrament is defined to be "a sacred performance whereby grace acts in a mysterious manner upon man. In other words, it is the power of God unto salvation." "The sacraments are divided into two classes: first, such as are absolutely necessary in themselves—namely, baptism, holy chrism, and communion. These are indispensably necessary for procuring salvation and eternal life; for it is impossible to be saved without them. The second division embraces those sacraments, the necessity for which proceeds from something else."

3. "The benefits conferred by baptism are the remission of original sin, the remission of all past actual sins, and grace to sustain the believer in his conflict with the world, the flesh and the devil."

2. *Anglican Church.* The thirty-nine Articles which form the standard of faith in the Anglican Church give no formal definition of the "Holy Catholic Church." Bishop Pearson, in his book on the creed, furnishes such a definition, as follows: "The single persons professing faith in Christ are mem-

FORMAL DEFINITIONS

bers of the *particular churches* in which they live, and all these particular churches are members of the general and *universal Church,* which is *one by unity of aggregation,* and this is the Church of the creed which we believe, and which is in other creeds expressly termed one, 'I believe in the Holy Catholic Church.'" The "particular churches" here referred to, composing the Church universal by "aggregation," are specified in Article XXXIV. as "national churches."

The English Parliament of 1532 declared England to be "an empire made up of spirituality and temporality [lords spiritual and temporal]" ("Church and Age," I: 17).

As to what constitutes a "visible church," we learn from Article XIX. that it is "a congregation of faithful men, in the which the pure word of God is faithfully preached and the sacraments be duly administered according to Christ's ordinances, in all those things that of necessity are requisite to the same."

The "due administration" of the sacraments, again, depends upon the validity of the ordination of the administrant by a bishop in the line of historically continuous succession from the apostles. (So Bishop Pearson, "On the Creed," Art. IX.)

The sacraments, so administered, are essential to salvation. Article XXVII. says of baptism: "It is also a sign of *regeneration* or new birth, whereby, *as by an instrument,* they that receive baptism rightly are grafted into the Church. . . . The baptism of young children is in anywise to be retained in the Church, as most agreeable with the institution of Christ."

The baptismal formula in the "Book of Common Prayer" prescribes the following prayer after the baptism of an infant: "We yield thee hearty thanks, most merciful Father, that it hath pleased thee *to regenerate* this infant with thy Holy Spirit, to receive him for thine own child by adoption, and to incorporate him into thy holy Church," etc.

II. SUMMARY OF COLLEGIATE THEORY.—The essential ideas underlying this theory are:

1. *Divinely instituted territorial rule.* The Church being the earthly manifestation of the Kingdom of heaven, its chief officials must be "kings" as well as "priests." Every priest is supreme in his own parish, sub-

FORMAL DEFINITIONS

ject only to the bishop of his diocese, who, again, is subject to no one but the primate or the patriarch, he in turn being responsible to no man but to Christ only. All citizens of his territory are *ipso facto* his subjects.

2. *Grace thorugh external sacraments only.* There being no salvation outside the Church, and the Church being a visible body, it follows that admission to it and to its benefits must come through visible channels. Regeneration and inclusion in the Church come, accordingly, *ex opere operato,* through lawfully given baptism, and sanctification through the eucharist.

3. *Unbroken continuity in transmission of apostolic gifts.* The validity of the sacrament depends on the genuineness of the transmitted authority of the administering priest. This authority being a concrete thing, literally passing by manual transfer, must be historically proven in order to security of imparted grace. The longing for this unquestionable historic continuity drove J. H. Newman to the Church of Rome, and has led to the recent effort of English clergy to secure from the Pope an endorsement of their priestly legitimacy. Determined not to

THE CHURCH AND THE KINGDOM

be defrauded at this point, "for centuries in the church of Alexandria, and still in the church of Armenia, the dead hand of their first bishop" is applied to the head of the new priest in ordaining him.

4. *Unity as a world power.* This theory agrees with the imperial in tracing all power to an apostolic origin. It differs only in making the college of apostles, rather than Peter alone, the center of unity. In the Eastern and Anglican, as well as in the Romish Church, there is an ascending hierarchy from priest to archbishop or patriarch, each grade being subordinate to, and receiving authority from, that above it. This gradation corresponds with, and (as the names of its territorial area, beginning with the *paroikia* or parish, suggests) was derived from, the organization of the Roman Empire. But, while the former two stop with the patriarch or primate, corresponding with the secular prefect, the Romish Church completes the parallelism with the empire by adding the supreme ruler in the pope, who became, like the emperor, Pontifex Maximus. Rome thus simply completes the same pyramid which England and the Orient leave truncated.

FORMAL DEFINITIONS

III. LOGICAL SEQUENCES OF THEORY.

1. *As to the religious life.*

(1) The sensuous element rules. In the Eastern Church the baptized infant is at once given the bread and wine of the eucharist, thus being sanctified as well as saved by sacramental means (Stanley, "Eastern Church," 118). In the same church it requires twenty folio volumes to direct the details of ritual for specific occasions (Lewis, "Bible, Missal," etc., 16).

Council of Moscow, 1656, "invoked heavy curses on all who presumed to make the sign of the cross with two fingers instead of three" ("Am. Cath. Quarterly," 1890).

Tractarianism in England laid equal emphasis on importance of position at the altar, details of vestment and genuflection and the like.

(2) Fossilization in thought and indifference in morals have followed. The Greek Church calls itself the "Holy Orthodox," and clings to antiquated dogmas and routine. As at Rome, "religion" is the affair of the priest or the monk. The layman has no need or right to think, but only to submit. He need not concern himself about his sins so

THE CHURCH AND THE KINGDOM

long as they can be officially forgiven at small cost.

Ritualism everywhere supplants spirituality. The great cathedrals are the work of the darkest period of the Middle Ages. Moscow is a city of churches, monasteries, shrines and images, but also of crime and debasing influences. "Israel hath forgotten his Maker, and builded temples."

2. *As to civil and religious liberty.*

(1) The voluntary factor is excluded. Every babe born into the realm is born *de jure* a member of the national church. Normally he must be in infancy made *de facto* a member by baptism.

Hooker, in his "Ecclesiastical Polity" (Oxford, 1843), II. 386 (Book VIII., Sec. 1), writes: "There is not any man of the Church of England but the same man is also a member of the commonwealth, nor any member of the commonwealth who is not also a member of the Church of England." Wilson, in his essay on the "National Church," in the famous "Essays and Reviews," confirms this notion as follows: "Each one born into the nation is, together with his civic rights, born into a membership or privilege as belonging to a spiritual

FORMAL DEFINITIONS

society." Dean Fremantle, in his recent work on the "World as Subject of Redemption," adds that in England "there is no established church, but only an established clergy—the nation is the church."

(2) External conformity may therefore be properly required and dissent suppressed. External worship can only be controlled by force. The prohibition and persecution of nonconformists to secure national unity of worship has been common in churches holding the theory in question. "No bishop, no king," said James I., and he proceeded to compel submission to the bishop. The Czar of Russia becomes a priest and head of the Russian Church. King George is supreme custodian of the offices of the church and of its worship in England. Dissenters exist only by his sufferance.

III.

THE SACRAMENTAL THEORY

I. DEFINITIONS.

1. *Lutheran.* Luther's Catechism (1529) substitutes the word "Christian" for "catholic" in the Apostles' Creed, and adds the following interpretation of the term: "The Creed calls the 'Church' a 'communion of Saints'—a term perfectly equivalent; meaning, as the clause should be rendered, a Christian community or congregation, or most appropriately a holy Christendom. For this clause was added as explanatory of what goes before, defining what the Church is; viz., a holy community on earth, composed only of holy persons, real saints, under one head, Christ, called together by the Holy Ghost, in one faith, mind and judgment, endowed with various gifts, yet concordant in love, free from heresy or schism."

The *"Confessio Helvetica,"* originally published in 1536, with the express endorsement of Luther and other theologians

FORMAL DEFINITIONS

standing with him, reissued in revised form in 1566, reads as follows (Art. XVII.): "Since God would have all men from the beginning to be saved, and to come to the acknowledgment of the truth, there must needs always have been, be now, and exist hereafter, even to the end of the world, a Church, that is, a congregation of faithful men called out, or gathered, from the world —a communion of saints— of those, namely, who truly know and rightly worship, through the word and the Holy Spirit, the true God in Christ. It is of these—the fellow-citizens of the saints and of the household of God, sanctified by the blood of the Son of God— that the article of the Creed, 'I believe in the Holy Catholic Church, the communion of saints,' is to be understood."

The *"Confessio Saxonica,"* drawn up by Melancthon (1551), in its ninth article, after reiterating substantially the same idea last cited, adds: "We do not speak of the Church as a Platonic idea, but we point out the Church which can be seen and heard. We, therefore, say that the *Church invisible* on earth is the congregation of those embracing the gospel and *rightly using the sacraments, in which,* through the ministry of the gospel,

THE CHURCH AND THE KINGDOM

God regenerates many unto life eternal; in which congregation there are, nevertheless, many who are not saints" (McElhinney, "Doct. of Church," 147-150).

In the Augsburg Confession of 1530, which continues the common standard of faith among the various branches of the Lutheran Church, the following definition is given; viz., "Art. VII. Also they teach, that *one holy Church* is to continue forever. But the Church is the *congregation of saints* (the assembly of believers), in which the gospel is rightly taught (purely preached), and the *sacraments rightly administered* (according to the gospel).

"And unto the *unity of the Church,* it is *sufficient* to agree concerning the *doctrine* of the gospel and the administration of the *sacraments.*"

As to the *sacraments* themselves, we read in Article V. that "by the Word and *Sacraments,* as by *instruments,* the *Holy Spirit is given;* who worketh faith, where and when it pleaseth God, in those that hear the gospel. . . . They condemn the Anabaptists and others, who imagine that the Holy Spirit is given without the outward Word, through their own preparations and works"

(Jacobs, "Book of Concord," I: 38, 39).

In Article IX. it is said: "Of *Baptism* they teach that it is *necessary to salvation,* and that *by Baptism* the *grace of God* is *offered,* and that *children* are to be *baptized,* who, *by Baptism* being offered to God, are *received into God's favor.* They *condemn* the *Anabaptists,* who allow not the baptism of children, and *affirm* that *children are saved without Baptism*" (Jacobs, *u. s.* 40).

Again, in the Small Catechism (Part IV.), in answer to Question II., "What gifts or benefits does Baptism confer?" it is answered: "It *worketh forgiveness* of sins, *delivers from death* and the devil, and confers *everlasting salvation* on *all who believe* as the Word and promise of God declare" (Jacobs, *u. s.* 370).

Coming to infant baptism, in the Large Catechism we read: "Here we are brought to a question by which the devil, through his sects, confuses the world . . . *whether children also believe,* and it be right to baptize them?" To this doubt it is replied that "even though infants *did not believe,* which, however, is not the case (as we shall now prove), yet their *baptism would be genuine,* and no one should rebaptize them."

THE CHURCH AND THE KINGDOM

The "proof" thus proposed to be given (of faith in the child) seems to be this: "We bring the child in the *purpose and hope* that it *may believe,* and we *pray* that God may *grant it faith:* but we do not baptize it upon that, but solely upon the command of God" (Jacobs, *u. s.* 471-2-3).

"Anabaptists pretend that children, **not as yet having reason, ought not to receive** baptism. I answer that reason in no way contributes to faith. Nay, in that children are destitute of reason, they are all the more fit and proper recipients of baptism. For reason is the greatest enemy that faith hath. It never comes to the aid of spiritual things, but—more frequently than not—struggles against the Divine Word, treating with contempt all that emanates from God. If God can communicate the Holy Ghost to grown persons, he can, a fortiori, communicate it to young children. Faith comes of the word of God, when this is heard. *Little children hear that word* when they receive baptism, and therewith they receive faith" (**Luther,** "Table Talk"—Phil., '68—p. 202).

As to the *right administration* of the sacraments, the Augsburg Confession (Art. XIV.) holds that "no man should publicly

FORMAL DEFINITIONS

in the church teach, or administer the sacraments, unless he be *rightly called*" (Jacobs, u. s. 41). But this does not necessarily involve episcopal ordination. On the contrary, the "Smalcald Articles" (Part II.) expressly *deny* the exclusive right of the *bishop to ordain*, claiming that the "authority to call, elect and ordain ministers ... is a gift exclusively given to *the church,* which no human power can wrest from the church" (Jacobs, *u. s.* 349).

2. *Methodist.* The Articles of Faith of the American Methodists were drawn up by John Wesley, and adopted here in 1784. They are an abridgment of the Thirteen Articles of the Anglican Church, from which all Calvinistic features are carefully effaced. Article XIII. is as follows: "The visible church of Christ is a congregation of faithful men, in which the pure word of God is preached, and the sacraments duly administered according to Christ's ordinance, in all those things that of necessity are requisite to the same" ("Discipline," 1876, p. 21).

Article XVI., concerning the *sacraments*, describes them as not only badges or tokens of Christian men's profession, but rather they are certain signs of grace, and God's good will toward us, *by the which he doth work invisibly in us, and doth not only quicken, but also strengthen and confirm, our faith in him.*"

Article XVII. says of baptism that "it is not only a sign of profession and mark of difference, *whereby Christians are distinguished from others that are not baptized;* but it is also a sign of regeneration or the new birth. The baptism of young children is to be retained in the Church."

In the "General Rules," Section 48, we find the following statement of the "Relation of Baptized Children to the Church:" "We hold that *all children, by virtue of the unconditional benefits of the atonement,* are members of the Kingdom of God, and, therefore, are graciously entitled to baptism."

Section 49 adds that "we regard all children who have been baptized as *placed in visible covenant relation with God,* and under the special care and supervision of the Church."

Section 52 further adds that "whenever baptized children have attained an age sufficient to understand the obligations of religion, and shall give evidence of piety, they may be admitted to *full* membership in

FORMAL DEFINITIONS

our church, on the recommendation of a leader with whom they have met at least some months in class, by publicly assenting before the church to the Baptismal Covenant, and also to the usual questions on Doctrines and Discipline" ("Discipline," 1876).

This rule has been modified since the publication of the "Discipline" in 1864. It is there provided that baptized children, on giving "evidence of a desire to flee from the wrath to come, and to be saved from their sins," should, "with their own consent, be enrolled on the *list of probationers,* and if they shall continue to give evidence of a principle and habit of piety, they may be admitted into full membership," etc. ("Discipline," 1864, Gen. Rules, Ch. II., Sec. 2, Q. 3).

The office of bishop, as defined in Sections 155-160 ("Discipline," 1876), gives him no territorial and no civil authority, but makes him a traveling superintendent of church work, who needs neither apostolic succession nor even exclusive episcopal consecration to give validity to his functions; the office itself not being essential in the polity of the church.

THE CHURCH AND THE KINGDOM

Whatever question may now arise as to the interpretation of the statement in Articles XVI. and XVII., that the sacraments *"work invisibly* in us," there can be no question as to the meaning of the phrase in the mind of Mr. Wesley, who originally placed it in the "Articles." In his "Treatise on Baptism" (Works—N. Y., '50—Vol. VI., 12-22) he sums up the benefits of baptism as follows: 1. It *"washes away the guilt of original sin,* by the application of the merits of Christ's death." So that "it is *certain,* by God's word, that children *who are baptized, dying before they commit actual sin, are saved."* 2. "By baptism we enter into *covenant with God* . . . that *new covenant* which he promised to make with the spiritual Israel; even to *'give them a new heart* and a new spirit, to sprinkle clean water upon them (of which the baptismal is only a figure) and to *remember their sins* and iniquities *no more.'"* 3. "By baptism we are *admitted into the Church,* and consequently *made members of Christ, its head."* 4. "By *water,* then, *as a means,* the *water of baptism,* we are *regenerated or born again;* whence it is called by the apostle 'the washing of regeneration.'" 5. "In consequence of our being

FORMAL DEFINITIONS

made children of God, we are *heirs of the Kingdom* of heaven."

As to the need of baptizing infants, he concludes that "if infants are guilty of original sin, then they are the proper subjects of baptism; seeing, in the ordinary way, they *can not be saved, unless this be washed away by baptism.*"

II. SUMMARY OF SACRAMENTAL THEORY.—The central propositions that underlie this theory, and differentiate it from the others thus far considered, are the following:

1. *The true Church universal is invisible as to organization.* Luther insisted that the "Holy Catholic (Christian) Church," referred to in the Apostles' Creed, is there expressly defined by the following parallel phrase as "the communion of saints." This inward fellowship is invisible. The *earthly* "Kingdom of heaven" is a "kingdom within." The only ruler in it is the invisible Christ.

2. *The alleged sovereignty of Peter or of the college of apostles; and their exclusive custody of divine grace, and power to transmit it by continuous touch to their successors, are all fictitious.* The appendix to the "Smalcald Articles" (Jacobs, *u. s.* 338-352)

is very full on this head. For instance, it cites the language of Paul in 1 Cor. 3: 6, as proving that "ministers are *all equal,* and that the *church* is *above the ministers."* "Hence superiority or lordship over the church or the rest of the ministers is not ascribed to Peter. For he says, 'All things are yours; whether Paul, or Apollos, or Cephas;' *i. e.,* let not other ministers assume for themselves lordship or authority in the church."

The General Conference of the Methodists in America (1784) received Thomas Coke, who had been consecrated as a bishop by John Wesley (himself not a bishop), and Francis Asbury, who had in turn been consecrated by Coke, "being fully satisfied as to the validity of their episcopal ordination" ("Discipline," 1876, 15). Apostolic succession was thus ignored.

3. *The claim of episcopal or other ecclesiastical rule over any territory, or over civic affairs, is unwarranted.* In Article XXVII. of the Augsburg Confession (Jacobs, *u. s.* 62) it is laid down that "the *ecclesiastical* power concerneth *things eternal,* and is exercised *only* by the ministry of the *Word* and of the *Sacraments;* . . . the *political*

FORMAL DEFINITIONS

power is occupied about *other matters* than is the gospel. The magistracy defends not the minds, but the *bodies,* and *bodily things,* against manifest injustice; and *coerces* men by the sword and corporal punishments, that it may uphold justice and peace. Wherefore the ecclesiastical and civil powers are *not to be confounded."*

The Methodist "Articles" (XXIII.) declare the United States to be "a sovereign and independent nation" which "ought not to be subject to any foreign jurisdiction," and exhort *all* Christians to be "subject to the supreme authority of the country where they may reside." The functions of a bishop, as defined in Sections 155-160, confine him to exclusively ecclesiastical affairs.

4. *Uniformity in administration of the sacraments, as channels of saving grace, is made the only visible token of unity.* In Article VII. of the Augsburg Confession, above cited, it is expressly stated that "unto the *true unity* of the Church, it is sufficient to agree concerning the doctrine of the gospel and the administration of the *sacraments,"* it being essential that the latter be *"rightly administered."* It is further claimed in Article VIII. that entrance into the vis-

ible communion of the universal Church is effected by the sacrament itself, independent of the character of him who administers it; so that it is of itself the only absolute bond of external unity.

The Methodist Article XVII. makes baptism the *"mark of difference, whereby Christians are distinguished from others that are not baptized."* In Rule 51 baptized children are described as *"children of the Church,"* and in Rule 52 they are spoken of as being on certain conditions "admitted into *full* membership in the Church;" implying that in some qualified sense they are *already members.* John Wesley even more explicitly makes baptism the one key to visible unity; for he affirms that by baptism we "are mystically united to Christ, and made one with him." For "by one Spirit we are all baptized into one body"; namely, the Church, "the body of Christ" (Works, VI., 15).

Rev. Dr. Newman, the well-known Methodist clergyman, during a camp-meeting at Ocean Grove, said: "As soon as a child is baptized, his name should be recorded on the church books, and he should be taught that he is just as much a Christian as he is an American citizen."

III. Logical Sequences of the Theory.

1. *Confusion as to the doctrine of salvation by faith alone.* The Anabaptists confronted Melancthon with the proposition that if salvation depended solely on faith, an internal experience, it could not at the same time depend on baptism, an external act; and that, in Scripture, baptism is made the personal and voluntary duty of a believer only, and could not, in such case, be rightly administered to an unconscious babe. He thereupon wrote Luther that they had "touched him in a sore place, and he knew not how to answer them." Luther, in reply, fell back on the authority of long-established custom, and, while admitting that faith must normally precede baptism, contented himself with the suggestion that as "faith is the gift of God," he must be assumed to give it to babes, even unconsciously, when asked.

The Methodists also, taking over infant baptism from the Anglican Church, with John Wesley's corresponding notion of full "grafting into the Church" derived from the same source, have found it embarrassing to maintain, at the same time, the necessity of personal and conscious regeneration before admission to the privileges of church membership. According to the "Discipline" of 1864, full membership was denied to baptized children, and they were required to become probationers at their own request. There came to be this anomalous condition of things. Children who had, according to Article XVII., become "Christians" by baptism, were now required to become "probationers," and so put on the same footing with those who, not having been baptized, were still non-Christians; and both were required to take the same steps to become full members. Infant baptism was thus practically nullified, while still theoretically insisted upon.

2. *Formalism stagnating thought and eating out spirituality.* The notorious decline of the German people from the evangelical doctrine and from the spiritual earnestness of the Reformers has been attributed by her foremost theologians primarily to the prevalence of infant baptism, with its inevitable implication of sacramental grace. The minister has there again become practically a priest, and men are saved, not by the "regeneration that washes," but by the "washing that regenerates."

Professor Tholuck said to Joseph Cook:

FORMAL DEFINITIONS

"I regret nothing so much as that the line of demarcation between the Church and the world, which Jonathan Edwards and Whitefield drew so deeply in the mind of New England, is almost unknown, not to the theological doctrines, but to the ecclesiastical forms of Germany. With us confirmation is compulsory. Children of unbelievers, as well as of believing families, must, at an early age, be baptized and profess faith in Father, Son and Holy Ghost.

"Without certificate of confirmation in some church, employment can not be legally obtained. After confirmation the religious standing is assumed to be Christian. After that we are all church-members. Thus it happens that in our state church the converted and unconverted are mixed pell-mell together" ("Bib. Sac.," 32: 739, 740). In a few cities of North Germany licenses were granted to women for an infamous profession, but only on exhibition of certificates of confirmation.

In the Methodist Church, Wesley's earnest emphasis on the necessity of the experimental element in religion (inconsistent as it manifestly was with his own doctrine of baptismal regeneration) has brought about

THE CHURCH AND THE KINGDOM

the incongruous attitude of the later church toward baptized children above mentioned. His influence has also issued, apparently, in relative disparagement of doctrine on the one side, and a present tendency to ritualistic development on the other.

In the *Literary Digest* for Nov. 13, 1897, is an account of a recent address by Bishop Goodsell, of the Methodist Church. He there says that no one can keep his ear close to the voices of the church without hearing two movements in opposite directions.

"One is toward the modification, if not destruction, of all which indicates our descent from the Church of England; the other seeks to assimilate our worship and the plan of our episcopal supervision to that from which our fathers came out. For a moment let us recall our history. We receive from that church our Articles of Religion, our ritual, our ministerial orders and office; and from her Arminian divines our theology. But we are not the heirs of her spirit. . . .

"The case is different with regard to the enrichment of the church's mode of worship and possibly with regard to the localization of the episcopate. Toward these, decided advance has been made of late. Three items

FORMAL DEFINITIONS

in the English service have been formally placed in the order of worship; namely, the recitation of the Apostles' Creed, the responsive reading of the Psalms, and the *Gloria Patri* thereafter. The use of these is now directed by the supreme body of the church, and the bishop thinks that the time is near when additional liturgical elements should be allowed to such congregations as desire them."

3. *Relation of Church and State.* Episcopacy is not reckoned theoretically an essential part of either Methodist or Lutheran organization. Where it prevails it carries no monarchic power. Luther's resentment of the Papal claim of supremacy over civil rulers was intense. He protested against the intrusion of the ecclesiastic into the realm of force, and equally against the counter intrusion of the rule of force into religious affairs. But *infant baptism* is itself an *intrusion of force* into religion, and, if essential to salvation, it logically suggests that the fatherly ruler see to it that his incipient subjects be early baptized. Actually, therefore, such baptism has become a legal requirement in Germany; and a certificate of baptism must be produced to secure license

THE CHURCH AND THE KINGDOM

to engage in lawful employment—as already shown. Religious liberty has in some Lutheran states been for a time almost or quite destroyed.

Sacramentalism thus insidiously leads to practical results of most inconsistent and harmful character . Its advocates, sooner or later, stultify themselves. They either are led by it into the renunciation of other radical opinions, or are led, by insisting on those opinions, to the practical, but unrecognized, abandonment of sacramentalism itself.

Grant ("Christendom"—New York, 1902): "Up to 1858 in Sweden no dissenting service was allowed; no Swedish citizen was allowed to secede from the state church" (410).

"In 1860 religious liberty (in part) was granted, since increased. The king, ministers of state, clergymen and religious teachers at state schools must be *Lutherans*. No cloisters or heathenish rites are permitted. No secession from Lutheranism is permitted (except actually to enter dissenting body). Dissenters must help support state church and state schools. The *king* is *head* of the church" (411).

"Religious liberty in Norway began

FORMAL DEFINITIONS

(1842) with abolishing law against conventicles. Norwegians may now leave state church and form separate congregation. (But Jesuits not allowed in the country.) King, ministers of state and public-school teachers must be Lutherans" (417).

IV.

THE HEREDITARY THEORY

Protestantism soon fell apart into two bodies, the conservatives clinging to Luther, while the so-called Reformed churches followed Calvin. The Lutheran Church of to-day is still the conservative body. Calvinism is represented by the Reformed, the Presbyterian, and (with notable qualifications) by the Congregational churches. The characteristic peculiarities of Calvinism were its emphasis on election as determining the constituency of the Church, and denial of sacramental power to "christen," or impart grace to any of the non-elect.

Commenting upon the phrase "the Holy Catholic Church," in the Apostles' Creed, Calvin declares that it includes "not only the visible Church, . . . but likewise all the elect, including the dead as well as the living."

In his Tracts (Vol. II., 115, ed. '49) he says: "Though the children of believers are

FORMAL DEFINITIONS

of the corrupt race of Adam, he [God] nevertheless accepts them *in virtue of this covenant* (to be "our God and the God of our seed to a thousand generations"), and adopts them into his family."

In the same volume (p. 338) he adds: "Did not God *transmit his grace from parents to children,* to admit new-born children into the Church would be a mere profanation of baptism."

Again, in the same volume (p. 87) he leaves no doubt of his belief in the sacramental efficacy of baptism when restricted to those thus rightly born; for he says: "It is certain that both pardon of sins and newness of life are offered to us in baptism and received by us."

In how far these ideas are still theoretically cherished by the Calvinistic bodies above specified will appear on consulting the language of their accepted standards, and their interpretation by representative leaders of each.

I. Definitions.

1. *Reformed churches.* The Reformed churches in America were formerly organized into two separate bodies: one called the Reformed Dutch; the other, the Reformed

German. Of these, the former accepted as its standard of faith the Belgic Confession, and the canons of the Synod of Dort (Schaff, "Creeds, etc.," III., 581). The latter clung to the Heidelberg Catechism.

In the Belgic Confession, 1561 (Revised 1619), the definition of the Church is as follows:

Art. XXVII. "We believe and profess one catholic or universal Church, which is a *holy congregation* and *assembly* of true Christian believers, expecting all their salvation in Jesus Christ, being washed by his blood, sanctified and sealed by the Holy Ghost.

"The Church *hath been* from the *beginning* of the world, and will be to the *end thereof;* which is evident from this, that Christ is an eternal *King,* which, without subjects, he can not be. . . .

"Furthermore, this holy Church is not confined, bound or limited to a certain place or to certain persons, but is spread and dispersed OVER *the whole world;* and yet it is joined and *united with heart and will,* by the power of faith, in one and the same spirit."

Art. XXVIII. "We believe that since this holy congregation is an *assemblage* of

FORMAL DEFINITIONS

those who are saved, and *out of it* there is no salvation, that no person of whatsoever state or condition he may be, ought to withdraw himself, to live in a separate state from it; but that all men are in duty bound to *join and unite* themselves with it, maintaining the unity of the Church," etc.

Art. XXIX. "The marks by which the true Church is known are these: If the pure doctrine of the gospel is preached therein; if she maintains the pure administration of the sacraments as instituted by Christ; if church discipline is exercised in punishing sin—in short, if all things are managed according to the pure word of God, all things contrary thereto rejected, and Jesus Christ acknowledged as the only Head of the Church. Hereby the true Church may certainly be known, from which no man has a right to separate himself. . . ."

As to hereditary right, it is said in Article XXXIV.: "We believe that every man who is earnestly studious of obtaining life eternal ought to be *but once* baptized with this only *baptism,* without ever repeating the same: since we can not be *born twice.* . . . Therefore we detest the error of the Anabaptists, who are not content with the one only baptism they have once received, and moreover condemn the baptism of the infants of believers, who, we believe, ought to be baptized and *sealed* with the *sign of the covenant,* as the children in Israel formerly were *circumcised* upon the *same promises* which are made unto *our children"* (Schaff, "Creeds, etc.," III., 417-425).

From the Canons of Dort (1618) we gather the following statement: Art. XVII. "Since we are to judge of the will of God from his word, which testifies that the *children of believers are holy, not by nature,* but in *virtue of the covenant of grace,* in which they together with the parents are comprehended, godly parents have no reason to doubt of the *election and salvation of their children* whom it pleaseth God to call out of this life in their infancy" (Schaff, III., 585).

In the Heidelberg Catechism (1563) Question 54 asks: "What dost thou believe concerning the Holy Catholic Church?" The answer is: "That out of the whole human race, from the beginning to the end of the world, the Son of God, by his Spirit and Word, gathers, defends and preserves for himself unto everlasting life, a *chosen communion* in the *unity of the true faith;* and

FORMAL DEFINITIONS

that I am, and forever shall remain, a living member of the same."

Question 69: "How is it signified and sealed unto thee in holy Baptism that thou hast part in the one sacrifice of Christ on the cross?" Answer: "Thus: that Christ has appointed this *outward washing* with water and has *joined therewith* this promise, that I am *washed with his blood* and Spirit from the pollution of my soul, that is, *from all my sins,* as certainly as I am washed outwardly with water whereby commonly the filthiness of the body is taken away."

Question 74: "Are *infants* also to be baptized?" Answer: *"Yes;* for since they, as well as their parents, *belong to the covenant and people of God,* and both *redemption* from sin and the *Holy Ghost,* who works through faith, are through the blood of Christ *promised to them* no less than to their parents, they are also by *Baptism,* as a sign of the covenant, to be *ingrafted* into the *Christian Church,* and *distinguished* from the *children of unbelievers,* as was done in the Old Testament by *Circumcision,* in place of which in the New Testament *Baptism* is *appointed"* (Schaff, "Creeds, etc.," III., 324, 329, 330).

THE CHURCH AND THE KINGDOM

In commenting on this last answer, Dr. Bethune ("Lectures on Catechism"—N. Y., '64—II., 258) says: "The *church* is the *visible representative* of the *kingdom of God* on earth. As the *children* of a citizen *inherit, of course,* the citizenship, *so* does the child of a church-member, by actual descent, become *entitled to church membership* until he forfeits it by his own conduct."

2. *Presbyterian churches.* The Westminster Confession of Faith, still the recognized standard of Presbyterianism (issued in 1647), contains the following definitions:

Art. XXV. 1. "The catholic or universal church, which is *invisible,* consists of the whole number of the *elect,* that have *been,* are, *or shall be,* gathered into one, under Christ the head thereof: and is the spouse, the body, the fullness of Him that filleth all in all" (citing various passages from Ephesians and Colossians).

2. "The *visible* church, which is also *catholic* and universal under the gospel (*not confined to one nation* as *before,* under the law) *consists of all those throughout the world that profess the true religion, and of their children* (American edition has "together with their children"); and *is the king-*

FORMAL DEFINITIONS

dom of our Lord Jesus Christ, the house and family of God, *out of which there is no ordinary possibility of salvation.* . . .

4. "This *catholic church* hath been sometimes *more,* sometimes *less,* visible. And particular churches, *which are members thereof,* are more or less pure, according as the doctrine of the gospel is taught and embraced, ordinances administered, and public worship performed more or less purely in them. . . .

Art. XXVIII. 4. "Not only those that do actually profess faith in and obedience unto Christ, but also the *infants of one or both believing parents,* are to be baptized" (divers passages from Old Testament and New Testament cited). . . .

6. "The efficacy of baptism is not tied to the moment of time wherein it is administered; yet, notwithstanding, by the right use of this ordinance the *grace promised is not only offered,* but *really exhibited and conferred* by the Holy Ghost, to such (*whether of age or infants*) as that grace belongeth unto, according to the counsel of God's own will, in his appointed time" (Schaff, "Creeds, etc.," III., 657-9, 661-3).

The same ideas as to subjects and efficacy

THE CHURCH AND THE KINGDOM

of baptism are repeated in the Shorter Catechism (1647), in answer to Questions 91-5.

"Children born within the pale of the visible church, and dedicated to God in baptism, are under the inspection and government of the church, and are to be taught to read and repeat the Catechism, the Apostles' Creed and the Lord's Prayer. And when they come to years of discretion, if they be free from scandal, appear to be sober and steady, and to have sufficient knowledge to discern the Lord's body, they ought to be informed that it is their privilege and duty to come to the Lord's table" ("Presbyterian Directory for Worship," Ch. IX., § 1).

Professor Witherow, in his "Form of the Christian Temple" (ed., '89, 200-213), *identifies* the *Church* with the *Kingdom,* and, after the citation of divers passages from the Old Testament, as well as the New, asks: "Does any doubt exist in the mind of any intelligent person who has examined these passages, that the *aggregate of all Christian congregations*—that is, *all* in the world who *profess* the true religion—constitute, *along with their children,* what is called the *Universal* or *Catholic Church?* This body may be viewed in a *twofold* aspect,

FORMAL DEFINITIONS

either as consisting of *all* who *profess* to belong to Christ, or of *all* who *are* Christ's in reality. In one aspect it is called, for sake of distinction, the Church *visible,* because the *profession* of Christianity, which marks its members out from the world and binds them all together, is itself a *visible* thing; in another aspect it is called the Church *invisible,* because the bond of faith and love, which binds them all to Christ and each other, can not be seen by mortal eye. . . . The congregation of Christian people dispersed throughout the whole world is the *Church visible and catholic; that is, the kingdom* of Christ on earth."

As to the *invisible* Church, "the congregation of *all saved souls* is, in the highest and truest sense, the Church of Christ, *one, holy, catholic and apostolic*—the collective company of *those whom He loved,* and *for whom He gave himself,* and whom He will present spotless and perfect to the Father at the last day."

Dr. Hodge gives the following definitions:

1. The true or invisible Church, *as a whole,* consists of *the elect* (Eph. 5: 25-27).

2. The true or invisible Church *on earth* consists of *all believers.*

3. The profession of faith made by those who are *baptized,* or come to the table of the Lord, is a profession of true faith; *i. e.,* they are *presumptively* true believers ("Systematic Theology"—N. Y., '77—III., 545; Ch. XX., Sec. 9).

He adds: 4. The Church under the new dispensation continues identical with that under the old (Rom. 11: 16, 17, etc.).

5. The terms of admission into the Church before the Advent were the same that are required for admission into the Christian Church.

6. Infants were members of the Church under the Old Testament economy (Gen. 12: 3, and 17: 7).

7. There is nothing in the New Testament which justifies the exclusion of the children of believers from corresponding membership in the Church (Acts 16: 15, 33, etc.).

8. Children need, and are capable of receiving, the benefits of redemption ("Systematic Theology," III., 547-558).

As preliminary to this defense of infant baptism, he *defines the visible Church,* remarking that, in order to justify the baptism of infants, we must attain and authenticate

FORMAL DEFINITIONS

such an idea of the Church as that it shall include the children of *believing parents.* "The word 'church' is used in *Scripture* and in common life, in *many different* senses. 1. It means the whole *body of the elect,* as in Eph. 5:25. The church is often said to be in this sense the body, or the bride, of Christ, to be filled by his Spirit, etc.

2. "It means *any number of contemporary believers, collectively considered;* or *the whole* number of believers residing in *any one* country or district, *or throughout the world.* In this sense we use the word when we pray God to bless his *Church universal,* or his Church in any particular land.

3. "It is used as a collective term for the body of *professed believers* in any *one* city; as we speak of the *church of Jerusalem,* of Ephesus, or of Corinth.

4. "It is used of any number of professed believers bound together by a *common standard of doctrine* and *discipline;* as the Episcopal, the Presbyterian, the Lutheran or the Reformed Church. And

5. "It is used for *all the professors of the true religion* throughout the world, considered as united in the adoption of the same

THE CHURCH AND THE KINGDOM

general creea, and in common subjection to Christ. . . .

"In the present discussion, by the Church is meant what is called the *visible Church;* that is, (1) the *whole body* of those who *profess the true religion,* or (2) *any number of such professors* locally united for the purpose of the public worship of Christ, and for the mutual exercise of watch and care" ("Systematic Theology," III., 547).

The subject is again elaborately treated by Dr. Hodge in his "Discussions in Church Polity" (N. Y., '78). He there begins with the statement that "in that symbol of faith adopted by the whole Christian world, commonly called the Apostles' Creed, the Church is *declared to be* 'the communion of saints.' "

It is obvious that the Church universal, considered as the "communion of saints," (1) "does *not* necessarily include the idea of a *visible society organized* under one definite form. . . . There can be no *kingdom* without a *king,* and no *aristocracy* without a *privileged* class. There may, however, be a communion of saints without a visible head, without prelates, without a democratic cove. nant. . . .

2. "Again, the conception of the Church

FORMAL DEFINITIONS

as the communion of saints does *not* include the idea of any *external organization.* ... The *Church,* therefore, according to this view, is *not essentially a visible society;* it is not a corporation, which ceases to exist if the external bond of union be dissolved. It may be proper that such union should exist; it may be true that it always has existed; but it is not necessary. The Church, *as such, is not a visible* society" ("Polity," p. 5).

"If the Church is the 'communion of saints,' it *includes all saints;* it has *catholic unity, because* it embraces *all the children of God.* ... Wherever the Spirit of God is, there the Church is; and as the *Spirit* is *not only within,* but *without all external Church organizations,* so the *Church itself* can not be limited to any *visible society*" (*Ib.,* p. 27).

"Protestants teach that the *true Church is visible:*

1. "Because it 'consists of men and women, in distinction from disembodied spirits or angels.'

2. "Because its members manifest their *faith* by their *works*" (outward life).

3. "Because believers are, by their 'effectual calling,' *separated* from the world" (in the spirit of their life).

THE CHURCH AND THE KINGDOM

4. "The true church is *visible* in the external church, just as the *soul* is visible in the *body* . . . the *external church,* as *embracing all* who profess the true religion—with their various organizations, their confessions of the truth, their temples, and their Christian worship—make it apparent that the true church, the body of Christ, exists, and where it is. These are *not the church,* any more than the body is the soul; but they are its *manifestations* and its r*esidence*" (*Ib.,* pp. 56-58).

"The *Protestant distinction* between the church *visible* and *invisible,* nominal and real, is that which Paul makes between 'Israel after the flesh' and 'Israel after the Spirit' " (*Ib.,* p. 59).

"It is to be remembered that there were *two covenants* made with Abraham. *By the one, his natural descendants* through Isaac were constituted a *commonwealth,* an *external visible community.* By the other his *spiritual descendants* were constituted *a church.* The parties to the former covenant were God and the nation; to the other, God and his true people. . . . When Christ came 'the *commonwealth*' was *abolished,* and there was nothing put in its place. *The Church*

FORMAL DEFINITIONS

remained. There was no external covenant, nor promise of external blessings, on condition of external rites and subjection. There was a spiritual society with spiritual promises, on the condition of faith in Christ. ... The Church is, therefore, in its essential nature, a body of believers, and *not an external society,* requiring *merely external profession* as the condition of membership" (*Ib.,* 67).

As to heredity of church membership, notice the following from representative leaders of Presbyterian thought:

Dr. H. J. Van Dyke, in the *Presbyterian Review* of 1885 (VI., 62), says: "Children of professed believers ... are members of the visible church, and presumptively regenerate, upon the same grounds that their parents are." (Cites Westminster Confession and Catechism.)

"Baptized infants are *professing* Christians and members of the visible church in the same sense that their parents are, and we are *bound to admit to the Lord's* table all members of the visible church who express an intelligent desire to partake of it" (*Ib.,* VIII., 482; 1887).

John Hall, in "Questions of To-day"

(263), says: "The children are *born into the* Church. . . . It is a medieval superstition that represents the child as 'christened' or made a Christian in the rite: and the only reason why the baptized child does not sit at the Lord's table, of course, is the counterpart of the restraint on the vote of the American youth."

3. *Congregationalist definitions.* The Cambridge Platform of 1648 defined the "Church Catholic" as "the whole company of those who are elected, redeemed, and in time effectually called from the state of sin and death unto a state of grace and salvation in Jesus Christ" (Ch. II., Art. XII.).

Article II. says that "this church is either triumphant or militant. Triumphant, the number of them that are glorified in heaven; militant, the number of them who are conflicting with their enemies upon earth."

Article V. adds that "the state of the members of the militant visible church walking in order was either before the law, economical, that is in families; or under the law, national: or, since the coming of Christ, only congregational (the term 'independent' we approve not)."

In Chapter III. the "matter" of a visible

FORMAL DEFINITIONS

Church is defined to be "saints by calling" and "the *children of such, who are also holy.*"

As to formal organization, it is said in Chapter IV. that "saints by calling must have a visible political union among themselves, or else they are not yet a visible church." As a "body," a "building" or "house." . . . "Hands, eyes, feet and other members must be united, or else, remaining separate, are not a body. Stones, timber, though squared, hewn and polished, are not a house, until they are compacted and united: so saints, or believers in judgment of charity, are not a church, unless orderly knit together." This "knitting together" is then said to be properly effected by a "church covenant" (Walker, "Creeds and Confessions of Congregationalism," 204-208).

The Savoy Declaration, which Dr. Schaff reckons the "fundamental Congregational confession of faith and platform of polity," was issued in 1658, during the Cromwellian Protectorate. It assents in detail to the utterances of the Westminster Confession, except in certain particulars specified. This "Declaration" was adopted by the Congregationalists of America in the Synod of Boston, 1680, and incorporated in the Saybrook Platform in 1708.

The National Council of Congregationalists in 1871 issued the so-called Oberlin Declaration, which is very brief. Among its few articles we read: "They agree in the belief that the right of government resides in local churches, or congregations of believers, who are responsible directly to the Lord Jesus Christ, the one Head of the Church universal and of all particular churches; but that all particular churches, being in communion with one another as *parts of Christ's Catholic Church,* have mutual duties consisting in the obligations of fellowship" (Schaff, "Creeds, etc.," III., 719-737).

The so-called "Commission" creed of 1883 says, in Article XI. (referring to the "sacraments which Christ has appointed for his church"), that baptism is "to be administered to believers *and their children,* as a sign of cleansing from sin, of union with Christ, and of the impartation of the Holy Spirit" (Walker, "Creeds, etc.," 581).

It appears, thus, that as to the normal composition of the Church, and the grounds

FORMAL DEFINITIONS

on which infants are included, Presbyterians, Reformed churches and Congregationalists are substantially at one.

II. SUMMARY OF HEREDITARY THEORY.

1. *The Church universal is composed exclusively of the elect.* As such it is a historic prolongation of the Old Testament Church—the Israelitish race. Calvin held the doctrine of a limited atonement. The "church which Christ purchased with his own blood" is composed only of that predetermined number for whom he died. Since this can neither be increased nor diminished by the act or omission of man, the notion that saving grace is dependent upon sacerdotal or sacramental conveyance is repudiated. Baptism is the "seal," not the channel, of regeneration.

2. *The Abrahamic covenant is still in force, and still "runs with the blood."* Calvin repudiated the traditional interpretation of John 3:5 ("Except a man be born of water," etc.) as referring to baptism, and teaching regeneration thereby. But he desired to retain infant baptism, the justification of which had rested chiefly on that passage so interpreted. He therefore transferred the defense of the custom to another

ground. He made baptism in the Christian Church the divinely appointed counterpart of circumcision in Israel. It thus became the birthright of the child of the believer.

3. *Birth of Christian parentage is a presumptive evidence of election and effectual calling.* (See *ante*, p. 51.) All children of Abraham were genealogically "children of the covenant," and the objects of exclusive divine favor. That favor expresses itself in the "new covenant" by the gift of a "new heart." The language of 1 Cor. 7: 14 is held to teach that the children of believers are, as such, "holy." God's election being invisible, and parentage being visible, the latter is the only tangible test of the former. To be the child of a believer in the new dispensation is tantamount to being a child of Abraham under the old; and birth being itself in God's hands, such birth must be the appointed token of his purpose of grace.

IV. LOGICAL SEQUENCES OF THE THEORY.

1. *Serious embarrassment engendered.*

(1) As to interpretation of Scripture language. If the Abrahamic covenant be interpreted literally, how can it be extended beyond those who are literally the "seed of

FORMAL DEFINITIONS

Abraham"? But we are not of Abrahamic, nor even Semitic, stock. If, on the other hand, the true children of Abraham become such by faith, as Paul seems to teach, and as adults are supposed to do (though of unbelieving parentage), how can they become children of the covenant by birth apart from faith?

(2) As to application of the theory.

a. To remote descendants. The promise was not only to Abraham's children, but to his children's children indefinitely. The early New England Congregationalists were for a long time sharply divided over the request of believing grandparents for the baptism of their grandchildren, the intermediate parents not being Christian. Their seemingly rational request was at last denied.

b. As to collateral members of the household. The Presbyterian General Assembly was called upon in 1855 to decide whether the infant slaves of Christian masters might be baptized at the request of the head of the household. This was allowed, on the strength of the precedent in the house of Abraham, in which those "bought with money" were circumcised. As that proceeding included adults as well as infant, it would seem to justify the baptism of grown-up slaves, as well as their children, on the same application.

2. *Disparagement of Scriptural authority.*

(1) As to relative authority of Christ and tradition. It is admitted that Christ explicitly commanded the baptism of the believer. Such a claim is made by nobody as to infant baptism. Admitted to be only inferentially required and to be continued as an adopted custom. Yet the human custom, traditionally transmitted, is allowed to supersede and obstruct the voluntary observance of the divine ordinance as explicitly commanded. The word of God is thus subordinated to the "commandments of men."

(2) As to universal need of regeneration. If baptized children be "presumptively regenerate" (the Catechism justifying that view); if they are withheld from the Lord's table by lack of intelligence only and not of spiritual change—how can they be reasonably taught that they need to be "born again"? Dr. Horace Bushnell, in his "Christian Nurture," holds that it is a serious error not to persuade the believer's child

that he is already regenerate. But Nicodemus was a circumcised "child of the covenant," and it was to him that the pressing need of the new birth was commended by Christ himself.

3. *Confusion as to constituency of the church.* The uniform language of the creedal documents based upon the hereditary theory represents the Church as consisting of "believers and their children." Infants are alluded to as "born into the pale of the Church," as "birthright members," and otherwise entitled, *prima facie,* to all the rights of full membership.

Yet the Congregationalists, while using precisely as strong language on the subject as the Presbyterians, practically nullify its force by their opposite treatment of the subjects of the rite. Presbyterians, theoretically at least, insist that the "tares and wheat must grow together till the harvest"; and that children of believers, whether in fact regenerate or unregenerate, are "saints by calling"; *i. e.,* full members of the body. The Cambridge Platform defines the "matter" of the visible Church as "saints by calling," made up of those who have "by profession of their faith and repentance, and by their blameless walk, positively shown themselves such"; but also made up of "the children of such who are holy." Yet these same holy children, who were "born into the church," and have been "sealed" by baptism, must reach full membership by the same process of open profession as the unholy and unbaptized offspring of unbelievers. This effort to maintain the principle of a regenerate church membership, while clinging to the covenant theory, "gave much trouble to New England Congregationalists," says Professor Ladd, of Yale, in his "Principles of Church Polity" (N. Y., '82), 196.

Finally came the famous "Half-way Covenant," which Professor Walker styles a "half-way house between the church and the world." By it those baptized in infancy might, upon "owning the covenant"—that is, by assenting intellectually to the doctrines, and promising to conform to the rules, of the Church—be admitted to voting membership without sharing in the Lord's Supper, and might have their children baptized. This, again, led to further relaxation, so that the same persons, while still confessedly unregenerate, became full members. In the

FORMAL DEFINITIONS

end the worldlings, thus admitted, came to be a majority. They called pastors after their own heart, and Unitarianism thus gained a foothold and absorbed a large part of the property of the Congregational churches in New England. The subterfuges resorted to in argument by those who favored the "Half-way Covenant," says Professor Ladd ("Principles of Church Polity," 199), "are really distressing." Joseph Cook, himself a Congregationalist, says in his "Lectures on Orthodoxy" (p. 270 *seq.*) that "infant baptism was the germ of Unitarianism and skepticism in New England." Prof. G. F. Wright wrote in the *Bibliotheca Sacra*, 1874, a strong article on the subject, showing the peril of confusion of thought introduced by infant baptism.

4. *Uniting of Church and State and persecution of nonconformists.* Resort to the Abrahamic covenant by Calvin, in one particular, naturally drew on the whole Old Testament scheme of organization, and Geneva became a theocracy. Servetus was executed by the civic authorities, who, as ecclesiastics, had first condemned him for heresy. New England Puritans fleeing from the tyranny of the "lord bishops," estab-

THE CHURCH AND THE KINGDOM

lished what one of their victims called the "tyranny of the lord brethren." Baptists and Quakers were whipped and exiled for attempting to exercise that liberty of conscience to establish which the Puritans and Pilgrims had professedly come hither. The persecutors were sincere, but sincerely wrong and inconsistent. And this was logically traceable in great part to the determined retention of a perverted rite which has uniformly bewildered and stultified its devotees when so perverted.

The Congregationalists have stoutly asserted always that they sought to preserve a regenerate and voluntary church membership. They have as stoutly, in practice, insisted on a membership involuntary and mixed.

The hereditary theory thus leads into self-contradiction as well as contradiction of Scripture.

V.

THE VOLUNTARY THEORY

The theories thus far considered, while differing in various other details, all agree as to the normal constituency of the Church. It is made up of those who have, in infancy and without their own volition, been made members of it, whether by the hand of the priest, by the universality of Christ's redemptive work, or by birth into citizenship in a Christian state or into membership of a Christian household. Adult baptism is, indeed, recognized as valid, but treated as exceptional. For all persons who are entitled to a share in the ordinance, on whatever ground, ought to have been baptized in infancy; their later baptism, therefore, is abnormal, and permissible only as meeting an emergency improperly created by negligence of those responsible.

The Anabaptists of medieval times ("again baptists," as the word means etymologically), or "Anti-pedobaptists," as Dr. A.

H. Newman prefers to call them, stood alone against the remainder of Christendom in rejecting this conception, and insisting that the Church is legitimately to be made up only of those who have for themselves intelligently and voluntarily accepted Christ, obeyed his command in baptism, and asked for enrollment among his people. The great body of the Christian world still remains pedobaptist. Of those who follow the Anabaptist view, the so-called Baptists are the most influential representatives. Let us look at some of their standards in historic order, and some interpretations of them by their recognized leaders.

I. FORMULARIES.

1. *General, or Arminian, Baptist definitions.* (For the following citations, except as otherwise noted, reference may be made to the "Confession of Faith, etc., of Baptist Churches in England in the Seventeenth Century," edited by E. B. Underhill (London, '54).

The early, so-called Amsterdam Confession of 1611 defines the Church of Christ, in Article X., as follows: It is "a company of faithful people, separated from the world by the word and the Spirit of God, being

FORMAL DEFINITIONS

knit unto the Lord, and one unto another, by baptism, upon their own confession of the faith and sins."

Article XI. adds: "That though in respect of Christ the Church be one, yet it consisteth of divers particular congregations, even so many as there shall be in the world; every one of which congregations, though they be but two or three, have Christ given them with all the means of salvation, are the body of Christ," etc.

Article XIII. reads thus: "That every church is to receive in all their members by baptism, upon the confession of their faith and sins, wrought by the preaching of the gospel, according to the primitive institution and practice. And, therefore, churches constituted after any other manner, or of any other persons, are not according to Christ's testament" (Underhill, p. 6).

The so-called London Confession of 1660 makes *no allusion* to a *universal Church*. It defines the constitution of a local church as follows:

Art. XI. "The right and the only way of gathering churches, according to Christ's appointment, is first to teach or preach the gospel to the sons and daughters of men;

THE CHURCH AND THE KINGDOM

and then to baptize (that is, in plain English, to dip), in the name of the Father, Son and Holy Spirit, or in the name of the Lord Jesus Christ, such only of them as profess repentance toward God and faith in our Lord Jesus Christ. And as for all such who preach not this doctrine, but instead thereof that scriptureless thing of sprinkling of infants (falsely called baptism), whereby the pure word of God is made of none effect, and the New Testament way of bringing in members into the church by *regeneration* cast out: when, as the bondwoman and her son, that is to say, the O. T. way of bringing in children into the church by way of generation, is cast out, as saith the Scripture, all such we utterly deny; for as much as we are commanded to have no fellowship with the unfruitful works of darkness, but rather to reprove them" (*Ib.*, p. 113).

In their Confession of 1678 they cautiously define the *Church universal* thus:

Art. XXIX. "There is one holy catholic church, consisting of, or made up of, the whole number of the elect, that have been, are, or shall be, gathered into one body, under Christ, the only head thereof; *which church is gathered by special grace,*

FORMAL DEFINITIONS

and the powerful internal work of the Spirit; and are efficiently united unto Christ their head, and can never fall away."

Art. XXX. "Nevertheless, we believe the *visible* catholic church of Christ is *made up of several distinct congregations,* which make up that one catholic church or mystical body of Christ," etc. (*Ib.,* p. 149).

2. *Particular, or Calvinistic, Baptist definitions.* (These Baptists correspond to the so-called Regular Baptists of America as the General do to the Free Baptists.) This body presented to Parliament in England in 1646 a confession which was avowedly intended to show the Cromwellian party, then in power, that certain charges against them, of antagonizing the Westminster Confession, had been slanderously exaggerated. They aim to show how largely they agree and in what points alone they differ.

Article XXXIII. accordingly says: "Jesus Christ hath here on earth a spiritual *kingdom, which is his church,* whom he hath purchased and redeemed to himself as a peculiar inheritance; which church is a company of *visible* saints, *called and separated from the world by the word and Spirit of God,* to the *visible profession of*

THE CHURCH AND THE KINGDOM

the faith of the gospel, being baptized into that faith, and joined to the Lord, and each to other by *mutual agreement,* in practical enjoyment of the ordinances commanded by Christ, their Head and King." (The local church is thus really defined.) (*Ib.,* p. 39.)

The Confession of 1656 makes only the following allusion to the subject:

Art. XXIV. "That it is the duty of *every man and woman, that have repented from dead works,* and have faith toward God, to be baptized; that is, dipped or buried under the water, in the name of Our Lord Jesus, or in the name of the Father, Son and Holy Spirit. Therein to signify and represent a washing away of sin, and their death, burial and resurrection with Christ.

"And being thus planted in the visible church or body of Christ, who are a company of men and women separated out of the world by the preaching of the Gospel, do walk together in all the commandments of Jesus; wherein God is glorified, and their souls comforted." (Again a local church is described.) (*Ib.,* pp. 89, 90.)

The Confession of 1688 (known in this country as the Philadelphia Confession, because adopted by the Philadelphia Association early in the eighteenth century: since widely used) is preceded by an apologetic statement, explaining that its purpose is to correct certain misrepresentations which have greatly prejudiced the minds of others against them, they being still stigmatized as Anabaptists, which they strongly resent. They, accordingly, avow their purpose to follow the example of the Independents (or Congregationalists) in their Savoy Confession. They thus seek to "express their minds not only in words concurrent with the former (that is, the Westminster Confession) in sense, but also, for the most part, without any variation of terms. They have, therefore, made "use of the very same words with them both, in those articles (which are very many) wherein our faith and doctrine is the same with theirs." They are determined, they say, "to convince all that they have no itching to clog religion with new words."

Article XXV. adopts the language of the other two Confessions, the Westminster and Savoy, *substituting the word "kingdom" for "church" when speaking of the world-body:* Christ "shall always, notwithstanding the degeneracy of particular *churches,*" have "a *kingdom* in this world to the end thereof," of such as "believe in him, and make profession of his name."

Article XXVI., speaking of the invisible "catholic or universal church" of the other two Confessions, agrees that it consists of all the elect; but, instead of calling it "invisible" outright as they do, says "which (with respect to the internal work of the Spirit, and truth of grace) may be called invisible."

There is no article affirming a "visible catholic church." But the language of the Savoy Confession is followed in part, in the statement that "all persons throughout the world, professing the faith of the Gospel, and obedience unto God by Christ according unto it," etc., "are and may be called *visible saints*" (instead of the "visible catholic church of Christ," as in Savoy); adding, "*and of such ought all particular congregations to be constituted*" (*Ib.*, pp. 219, 220). The New Hampshire Confession of Faith (1833), the latest and probably most widely accepted of all among Northern Baptist churches, makes *no allusion* whatever to *a Church universal*, visible or invisible. It describes the local church only, under

FORMAL DEFINITIONS

the title "A Gospel Church" (in Art. XIII.). We there read as follows:

"We believe that a visible church of Christ is a congregation of baptized believers, associated by covenant in faith and fellowship of the Gospel; observing the ordinances of Christ, governed by his law and exercising the gifts, rights and privileges invested in them by his word" (Schaff, "Creeds, etc.," III., 746).

Turning to the voluminous literature in explanation and defense of the Baptist conception of the Church, it will be needful to make only two or three citations, especially as the subject will be further examined, directly, from the New Testament point of view.

Dr. W. R. Williams, one of the ablest of American Baptist writers, defines the New Testament church as "a local, independent, self-governed community . . . the original form of polity for the primitive Christian church." He adds that "some seem to forget this, and think of all the communities of primitive believers as making up but one visible church. To this new imaginary body it is easy to ascribe a legislation, a power of development and a power of depression and excision which the Holy Scriptures do not attach to churches as apostles move among them" ("Lectures on Baptist History," 95, 96).

Dr. T. Armitage says, in his "History of the Baptists": "In the apostolic age the church was a local body, and each church was independent of every other church. The simple term *ecclesia* designates one congregation, or organized assembly, this being its literal and primal meaning. . . . It follows, then, that the New Testament nowhere speaks of the 'Universal, Catholic, or Invisible, Church,' as indicating a merely ideal existence, separate from a real and local body. . . . A local church fully expresses the meaning of the word *ecclesia* wherever it is found in Holy Writ" (pp. 118-120).

II. SUMMARY OF VOLUNTARY THEORY.

1. *The definition of the Christian church must be derived solely from the New Testament.* All the Baptist symbols fortify their statements, one by one, by reference to New Testament passages, and rest exclusively on these. Defenders of other theories refer also to the same source, but lean in part on the Old Testament as well. They

FORMAL DEFINITIONS

base their practice, also, collaterally at least, on church authority, on ancient custom, and on expediency.

These latter hold that a church may be properly called Christian although only in part designed and molded by Christ. Baptists, on the contrary, insist that Christ alone is "King in Zion," to use one of their characteristic phrases.

2. *The term "church" in the New Testament primarily, if not exclusively, designates a local body.* Any more extended reference, such as to a "church universal," if real, is tropical only. This question will be discussed later and need not be here dwelt upon.

3. *The New Testament church was, and every Christian church ought in like manner to be, composed wholly of willingly baptized believers.* From the time of Augustine, sacramentarians and others have argued that, since "the tares and the wheat" must "grow together" until the harvest, a purely regenerate membership of the church is neither to be expected nor aimed at. One Anglican writer goes so far as to justify the bringing of unregenerate infants into the church by baptism, on the ground that "very few

of them would have embraced Christianity had it demanded individual conversion and personal effort." Congregationalists, on the other hand, have vigorously denounced the inclusion of the unregenerate in the church. Barrow, an early leader in that body, declared that "assemblies of good and bad together are no churches, but heaps of profane people." R. W. Dale, a modern Congregational leader, says (*"Ecclesia,"* II., 356): "Formally a religious society ceases to be a church when it ceases to require personal union with Christ as the condition of communion with itself, and when it consciously, voluntarily, and of deliberate purpose, includes within its limits what John Robinson, after the manner of his age, calls a mingled generation of the seed of the woman and the seed of the serpent." Yet, to this day, the Congregationalists insist in their formularies, that the church is composed not only of regenerate parents, but also of their (confessedly unregenerate) "households."

4. *The Christian church is purely voluntary in organization and maintenance.* The "covenant" is the only formal constitutional basis of Baptist, or other congregationally

FORMAL DEFINITIONS

governed, churches. Every member must for himself seek admission to the body, be accepted by its consent, and enter into mutual covenant with its members—the continuance of the relation being dependent on the continued assent of both parties. Into a church so constituted none can be legitimately thrust by priest, parent or irresistible predestination.

5. *The local church is subject, as are all its members, to the authority of Christ alone.* The Congregationalists were first called "Independents" in England. This was because of their assertion of the absolute independence of the individual church. Revolting against the assumed supremacy of pope, bishop, king, parliament, or other man of body of men, over the local church, they became "separatists" from the other Puritans as well as from the state church. But this radical idea, which gave them birth, had long been insisted upon by, and was probably borrowed from, the Anabaptists. Robert Browne, who is recognized as the father of English Independency, is admitted to have been early associated with the Dutch Anabaptists settled in Norwich, England. Curteis (in "Church of England and Dis-

THE CHURCH AND THE KINGDOM

sent," 71) insists that Browne learned his revolutionary ideas from them. Prof. W. Walker ("Creeds, etc.," 27, 35-6) confesses that the relationship is "difficult to deny," and recognizes the doctrine of churchly independence of state authority as an "Anabaptist" tenet, which Browne was the "first writer to proclaim in England." It remains to inquire whether Baptists and Congregationalists have been equally true in practice to this fundamental idea.

III. LOGICAL SEQUENCES OF THE THEORY.

1. *Individual responsibility to Christ emphasized.* Obedience is the other half of faith. If a child may render vicarious obedience to Christ's command to be baptized, how can we resist the logical inference that it may also vicariously believe? The responsibility for belief as well as for baptism is shifted in such a case to the shoulders of the magistrate, the priest, the parent, or the custodian, by whose act salvation is to be secured for those under their care. The Romish Church accordingly holds the sacrament to be efficacious through the faith of the priest alone. Luther held that faith may be unconsciously implanted, in sleep. The sponsor in the Anglican service professes

FORMAL DEFINITIONS

faith in the child's name. Presbyterian writers contend that, by virtue of the prior faith of one of their parents, children may be "sanctified from the womb," and that on a parent's becoming a believer his children, already born, may be thereby rendered "holy." The Congregationalists, clinging to the theory of "birthright membership," have, as we have seen, found it impossible to couple logically with it the incongruous idea of an exclusively regenerate church. Practice is apt to override and remold theory. The "Half-way Covenant" and the Unitarian apostasy were the logical outcome of the futile attempt to marry two incompatible theories—the false practice inevitably neutralizing and voiding the true doctrine. The Baptists, on the other hand, have consistently maintained that responsibility for acceptance of the authority of Christ and obedience of his command are alike personal, and can not be shifted to another. Maintenance of this view normally entails, of itself, a regenerate church membership, and involves no need of equivocal hypothesis or ingenious qualification of language in order to escape a dilemma. The Baptists, and their allies who repudiate pedobaptism, are the only consistent defenders of the voluntary idea.

2. *Unquestioning loyalty to Christ inculcated.* As a personal command requires personal obedience, so an unqualified command requires unqualified obedience. To evade or hinder such unhesitating response, by cavil as to a possible alternative meaning of words; by forbidding the right to ignore a supposed vicarious obedience already accomplished; by interposing ecclesiastical or traditional abolition or modification of an appointed rite, or by appealing to convenience or expediency or social relations as giving like sanction to change—is to derogate from the lordship of Christ and practically to set his explicit will at naught. The voluntary theory, therefore, consistently applied, must reject infant baptism, for it is admitted that Christ did not explicitly command it. It can therefore be no lawful substitute for the intelligently accepted baptism which he explicitly did command. *"Whatsoever* he saith unto you, do it," said the mother of Jesus, at the wedding feast. In like manner the Baptists loyally echo, "Do it," and not some other thing. Thus, and thus only, can the intrusion of the human, and the corresponding disparagement and

FORMAL DEFINITIONS

displacement of the divine, be avoided. It is not accident or perversity that connects the insistence upon immersion with the rejection of infant baptism. Loving loyalty to Christ demands exact conformity to his expressed will alike in either case.

It is needless to detail the evil results that have followed from tampering with the plain meaning of Christ's words; from the treatment of the thing commanded, acknowledged to be clearly defined, as, nevertheless, non-essential, and the like. Baptism and belief are constantly coupled in Scriptural command. If the one may be evaporated by verbal jugglery into indefiniteness of meaning or dismissed as non-essential, why may not the other be as legitimately dissolved into "shining ether," or peremptorily set aside as vain? One Congregationalist church not long ago broadened its conceptions of loyalty to Christ enough to take in a Unitarian church, which reckons neither faith in the authority of Christ nor baptism at his bidding as of serious consequence.

3. *Fraternal equality preserved.* As there is "no difference" in the status of the sinful, so there is no gradation in rank among the saved. They have "one Master, even

THE CHURCH AND THE KINGDOM

Christ," and all they are "brethren." The "princes of the church," "lord bishops," and all other hierarchical functionaries, assuming divinely imparted supremacy over the churches, as well as all other aristocratic or prelatic rulers in the local body, are excluded by the voluntary theory. Bogue and Bennett, in their "History of Dissenters," express surprise that Baptists, independent and variant as they have been in many things, have never adopted the episcopal or presbyterial polity. They do not seem to recognize the inevitable consequence of the Baptist conception of the nature of the church. If it has been constituted by, and rests upon mutual consent, then "every man must count for one, and no man for more than one," and absolute democracy results.

To say **nothing** of other bodies, there are even in the Congregational body at least three grades of membership, theoretically; and there were, at one time, four. For when the "Half-way Covenant" was in force there were infants unbaptized, but "holy"; infants baptized, but unresponsive as yet to the "covenant"; persons baptized in infancy who had later "owned the covenant," and been

FORMAL DEFINITIONS

admitted to certain church privileges; and, finally, the professedly regenerate. The first three classes were in some sense members (the terms "inchoate," "potential," "presumptive," "incipient," or other qualifying adjective, being used to designate their relative rank); but their exact *status* was always a matter of question. An entanglement again due to the effort to mix the incongruous.

4. *Religious l i b e r t y ensured.* Robert Robinson, of England, who wrote a history of the Baptists more than a hundred years ago, announced the legitimate outcome of the voluntary theory, fairly followed, in the following terms:

"The freedom of religion from the control of the magistrate; the simplicity and perfection of revelation without the aid of the scholastic theology; the absolute exemption of all mankind from the dominion of their clergy—are all included in the voluntary baptism of an adult, and in the maxim that the visible church which Christ hath established on earth is an assembly of true and real saints, and ought, therefore, to be inaccessible to the wicked, and exempt from all institutions of human authority. It is this maxim, with its contents, and not rebaptizing, that hath occasioned most of the persecutions of this party of Christians" (Benedict, "Hist. Baptists," p. 435).

In confirmation of these words may be cited the statement of Milman, an Anglican, that "infant baptism was one of the strong foundations of sacerdotalism." He adds that the early Anabaptists were "Biblical antisacerdotalists." Wall, in his "History of Infant Baptism" (p. 626), notes that "no state church has ever relinquished infant baptism." The German historian Gervinus, in his "Introduction" to the "History of the Nineteenth Century," credits the Anabaptists with being the "first advocates of that principle of religious liberty which brought the Pilgrims later to America." Skeats, in his "History of the Free Churches," characterizes the Baptists of England as the "proto-evangelists of religious freedom."

The Independents, with Robert Browne their leader, have often been claimed as the pioneers of this doctrine. But Skeats says (pp. 21, 34): "The first Independents adhered to the doctrine that it was the official duty of princes and magistrates to suppress heresy and root out all false religions and

FORMAL DEFINITIONS

counterfeit worship of God." Curteis, in his "Dissent, etc." (p. 69), says Browne "had no idea of what we now mean by toleration." The very title of Browne's work on "Reform without Tarrying for Any" implies as much; for those whose slow movements he would not await were the civic rulers.

The English Presbyterians openly advocated the union of church and state. The Westminster Confession declares that "they who, upon pretence of Christian liberty . . . shall maintain such erroneous opinions or practices as are destructive to the external peace and order of the church, may lawfully be proceeded against by the censure of the church and by the *power of the magistrate.*" The speedy and inconsistent lapse of New England Puritanism into persecution is evidence enough of the danger of departure from rigorous adhesion to voluntarism in religion, either in doctrine or practice. A recent writer says as to the "two swords" in New England: "Short as has been the interval between our own and colonial times, it has become difficult to get a clear and undistorted vision of the men and events of that era. There was so much incongruity in the temper and conduct of the

THE CHURCH AND THE KINGDOM

Pilgrims and Puritans themselves, that it is not wonderful to find assailant and defender each furnished with ample weapons for his purpose in their own history. They were 'separatists' from the Church of England for conscience' sake, but they would not endure 'separatists' from themselves. They limited the right of citizenship *to church-members,* and construed this to mean the avowedly regenerate alone; while t h e i r standards declared the Church to be constituted of believers and their offspring, including the unregenerate. They resented civil interference, on the part of the English authorities, in religious affairs, but had to be restrained from like interference by the English king."

# PART IV.
THE "HOLY CATHOLIC CHURCH"

I.

THE APOSTLES' CREED AS A BASIS OF UNITY

A feverish anxiety has of late become increasingly manifest that Christ should "restore at this time the kingdom to Israel." Sanguine evangelists have promised themselves that it is possible to Christianize the world "in this generation." Eager social reformers, reckoning the corporate regeneration of the social order as tantamount to, or, at least, the necessary precedent and immediate condition of the regeneration of the individual, have indulged in roseate hopes of a speedy economic and civic millennium. Meantime, the universal "fatherhood of God and brotherhood of man" have been formulated into a kind of working creed. New emphasis has been laid, among theologians, on the incarnation as, in effect, establishing a literal "solidarity" of the race.

In line with these general tendencies has appeared a quickened longing for the "re-

THE CHURCH AND THE KINGDOM

union of Christendom." The "Lambeth Proposals" for a consolidation of Protestantism under the "Historic Episcopate" have been followed by overtures to Rome for recognition of the legitimacy of Anglican Episcopal orders. Pan-Anglican, Pan-Presbyterian, Pan-Congregational, and other ecumenical conferences, have been convoked. National "federation of churches" for practical ends has been attempted. Nearly allied denominational bodies have consolidated. Interdenominational movements of divers kinds have been enthusiastically launched. The familiar words,

> "We are not divided;
> All one body we—
> One in hope and doctrine,
> One in charity,"

seem rather to irritate than inspire while they remain sentimental only. Men crave their palpable and permanent realization. But how is this to be promptly effected?

I. The Proposed "Talisman of Unity."—One of the most plausible of the suggestions toward this end was, sometime since, offered by the late distinguished rector of Grace Episcopal Church in New York City. He proposed the acceptance of the

THE "HOLY CATHOLIC CHURCH"

"simple terms" of the Apostles' Creed as a "talisman of unity" to rally the scattered forces of the "mighty army" of the "Church of God." This creed is already a part of the baptismal formula of the Latin, Anglican, Lutheran and Continental Reformed Churches. It is embodied in the Westminster Shorter Catechism. It is regularly recited in many Congregational churches. It is commended for weekly public use in the "People's Psalter," prepared for, and in many instances used by, Baptist churches. It is the doctrinal formula of the Evangelical Alliance.

Rev. Dr. H. A. Stimson, of the Congregational body, has expressed the belief that "the faith of the first century is to be the faith of the twentieth century"; since "the oldest extant Christian Confession that has any completeness is rapidly finding a new acceptance. It is heard to-day in public worship upon more lips than any form of words outside the Bible." The significance of this prophecy and the cogency of Dr. Huntington's suggestion lie in the assumption.

1. *That the creed in question is apostolic in origin.* If it embody the "faith of the

first century," it flows from near the fountain-head. Tradition once credited each of the apostles with having contributed a clause to it. This is an illusion now wholly abandoned, says Harnack; but the *"Catechismus Romanus"* still insists that the language of the creed is purely of apostolic origin. This, if true, would seem to give it an authority close akin to that of the New Testament, produced by the same hands. The New Testament being recognized as the tribunal of highest appeal, such an origin would make the document highly important as an aid to the interpretation of the words of the same writers in the New Testament itself.

2. *That the "Holy Catholic Church" is a definable historic reality.* It will be observed that all the theories of the Church, thus far examined (except the voluntary theory), agree in their reference to the actual or historic Church as "catholic"; that is, as world-embracing in comprehensiveness and single in nature. With one consent, therefore, they unite in professing faith in the "Holy Catholic Church." It is, of course, implied that "churches" are only to be spoken of in a tropical sense, as typical of or fractional parts of the "Church"

THE "HOLY CATHOLIC CHURCH"

proper, which is always ecumenical in range. But these assumptions prove, on examination, to be wholly unfounded. For

3. *Neither the creed itself nor the emphasized phrase are traceable to the first century.*

(1) The creed, in its present form, is affirmed by Harnack to be traceable no further back than to the middle of the fifth century. The "complete form of the creed," as Dr. Stimson admits, "gained general currency in the West" only "after the eighth century." The version in use before that time (itself going back only to the third century) omits the word "catholic," speaking only of the "Holy Church." That this was the earlier form is admitted by Romanists as well as Protestant historians.

(2) The word in question (catholic) is not applied to the Church in the Septuagint nor in the New Testament in a single instance. It is only inferentially, and therefore disputably, attached to it.

(3) Early Christian literature is equally innocent of any such application of the term.

The word is not to be found in any of the earlier formularies, nor is it used (in the ecumenical or comprehensive sense) in

THE CHURCH AND THE KINGDOM

any early writing. The term "Holy Catholic Church" does indeed appear in the letter of Ignatius to the Smyrneans, belonging (if genuine, which is still hotly disputed) to the second century. But F. C. Conybeare, who has made a special study of the literature of that place and time, insists that it is either a later interpolation or, of itself, proof that the document is not genuine. For that phrase "did not come into vogue until the latter half of the third century"; indicating that, if not interpolated, it shows the letter to be a "forgery of that date." He finds that the Armenian version of the letter (which is earlier than the Greek) uses, "instead of the obnoxious phrase, the simple and primitive expression we meet with in the Acts; viz., the 'churches' in such and such a region." But this is of small account, for in any case the word "catholic" is clearly not there used in the later sense of "ecumenical" or "universal." It was manifestly qualitative, implying catholicity of *doctrine*, and not quantitative, alluding to comprehensiveness of *extent*. The letter concerning the martyrdom of Polycarp, probably a contemporaneous document, alludes to the "Catholic church in Smyrna." This must,

THE "HOLY CATHOLIC CHURCH"

of course, refer to the orthodoxy or catholicity, in doctrine, of the body mentioned, which was local and not world-inclusive. Abundant evidence of the prevalence of this sense of the word among earlier Christian writers, limiting the idea of the "church" to the visible local body, might be given. The word "catholic" as applied to the church, and conveying the sense of a single world-body, was as yet foreign to the thought of the Christian community.

4. *The phrase in question, instead of being a "talisman of unity," evokes only discord.* While all join in the use of the same words, scarcely any two agree as to their meaning.

The Tridentine formulary *affirms*, while the Augsburg *denies*, the visibility of the "Holy Catholic Church"; but the Westminster Confession declares it to be *both* visible and invisible. According to the latter, it includes "the whole number of the elect, that have been, are, or shall be, gathered into one"; at the same time, it "consists of all those, throughout the world, that profess the true religion, and of their children." In the latter sense it is "catholic or universal" in that it is "not confined to one nation as before under the law" (which would seem to imply catholicity in *character* rather than extent). The Anglican Confession, in its nineteenth article, makes *"the* church" to be *"a* congregation"; implying a local and generic sense of the term "church" (as is clear from its further unequivocal use in Articles XXIV. and XXXV.); but in the same article reference is confusingly made to *"the* Church of Rome"; and in Article XXXIV. to "a particular or national church." The Oberlin Declaration holds the "catholic church" to be made up of "all particular churches" as "parts." The "People's Psalter" arbitrarily dissects out the phrase in question; substituting therefor the words "the church of the living God." The reciters of the creed, therefore, are discordantly professing accord in their common faith in a "Holy Catholic Church," of absolutely incoherent character. It must be a visibly organized world-power, and, at the same time, a purely mental creation; an aggregation at once of national corporations, of hereditary groups, of voluntary associations, and of individuals. It may be "catholic" in the sense of actual prevalence everywhere, or only in that of fitness to prevail. It may

THE "HOLY CATHOLIC CHURCH"

be limited to the unknown elect (being thus indeterminate in time and space), while it must also include elect and non-elect, voluntary and involuntary, in the determinate company of contemporary "professed" believers and "their children." The term has become, that is to say, *"vox, et præterea nihil."* The Augsburg Confession goes back to the phrase employed in earlier forms of the Apostolic Creed—the "holy Church." Luther, in his catechism, makes it the "holy Christian Church." The First Helvetic Confession declares that the "Holy Catholic Church" is "open and known to the eyes of God alone"; yet so distinctly recognizable by certain rites that without submission to these none can be reckoned as (without the special grace of God) belonging to it. Calvin, returning to the Old Testament, found visible unity again by help of the Abrahamic covenant, in making the Christian a prolongation of the Jewish organism; thus securing corporate continuity through heredity. In this he followed the Romish theory, excluding its political aspects only.

The Anglican Bishop Pearson, in commenting on the Apostles' Creed, defined the "Holy Catholic Church" as "one by unity of aggregation," "all particular churches being members of the general and universal Church." Bishop Blomfield, in his "Three Sermons on the Church," confirmed this judgment, claiming that all particular churches are "branches more or less profitable, more or less flourishing, of the one Holy Catholic Church." Strangely enough, the Congregationalists, in their Oberlin manifesto, have recently formulated a substantially similar formula, so far as literal terms go. Dr. Candlish, on the other hand, confidently treats it as settled that the Church consists solely of the "company of the elect forming the body of Christ." But, as to each of these definitions, according to the old proverb, "his neighbor cometh after and searcheth him." Dr. Hort, after careful scrutiny of the text, can find "not a word that exhibits the one *ecclesia* as made up of many *ecclesiæ*"; nor can he come upon any "evidence that St. Paul regarded membership of the universal *Ecclesia* as invisible, and exclusively spiritual, and as shared by only a limited number of the external *ecclesiæ;* those, namely, whom God has chosen." His own conception is that "to each local *ecclesia* St. Paul has ascribed a correspond-

THE "HOLY CATHOLIC CHURCH"

ing unity of its own: each is a body of Christ and a sanctuary of God: but there is no grouping of them into partial wholes or into one great whole. The members which make up the one *ecclesia* are not communities, but individuals. . . . The one *ecclesia* includes all members of all partial *ecclesiæ*, but its relations to them all are direct, not mediate." He significantly adds, as if afraid of being taken too literally in his definition of the word, that Paul's reference to the "one universal *ecclesia*," which occurs first in Ephesians, "comes from the theological, rather than from the historical side . . . it is a truth of theology and of religion, not a fact of what we call ecclesiastical politics."

Returning upon our track, we find it alternately affirmed and denied (1) that the universal Church is made up of particular churches; (2) that it is composed of the individual members of such p a r t i c u l a r churches; (3) that it is confined to the elect, independent of church relation altogether. If it be admitted, then, that Paul did have in mind a "universal" Church, it must still be left uncertain what kind of a Church he meant.

But, as to the matter of definition, we

are not yet at the end of confusion. Let us accept Bishop Pearson's formula, and we are instantly confronted with the inquiry, What is that "particular church" of which the Church universal is made up? Referring to the thirty-fourth of the thirty-nine Articles of the Church of England, we learn that "every particular or national church hath authority to change and abolish ceremonies," etc. In the nineteenth article of the same formulary occurs the statement that "the visible church of Christ is a congregation of faithful men in the which the pure word of God is preached, and the sacraments be duly administered according to Christ's ordinance, in all those things that are of necessity requisite to the same." It is further added, somewhat incoherently, that "as the churches of Jerusalem, Alexandria and Antioch have erred, so also the Church of Rome hath erred, not only in their living and manner of ceremonies, but also in matters of faith." The former of these articles would compel us to regard the universal Church as made up, under Bishop Pearson's definition, exclusively of national churches: since the "particular" is made synonymous with the "national." But the

THE "HOLY CATHOLIC CHURCH"

latter a r t i c l e clearly employs the term "church" in a distributive or generic sense: for it describes *"the* visible church of Christ" as *"a* congregation of faithful men"; *i. e., any* such congregation. Yet the addendum refers, in the same breath and without any explanation, to the "church of Rome," as if included in the same category of local bodies. This is incomprehensible, unless the reference be to the primeval church of Rome, which was such a single congregation. But it is more pertinent to our present inquiry to observe that it is, in these articles, made essential to the being even of the local church that "the sacraments be duly administered," etc. Such due administration is, by the English Church, reckoned absolutely impossible except at the hands of those who have been episcopally ordained. It follows, therefore, that no dissenting local body, to say nothing of its being non-national, can be acknowledged as a constituent of the Church universal. The Congregationalists could scarcely have intended to be measured, in their Oberlin use of terms, by the standard here indicated. It seems a little odd, in any case, that they should accept the title "Church Universal" as a fit designation of unconfederated local bodies throughout the world, while repudiating the name "Church Congregational" as describing the affiliated Congregational churches of America. Does mere geographical extension invert the meaning of words?

If we turn unsatisfied from the Episcopal to the *Presbyterian* definition of the Church universal, we shall encounter equally baffling cross-currents of opinion. Who are "the elect," referred to by Dr. Candlish (following the Westminster Confession) as composing the "one body of Christ"? The authoritative Melancthon cautions us against the delusion that any of the elect may be found outside the visible Church: the astute Charles Hodge assures us that visible individual saintship is the true criterion, wholly irrespective of church relation; while Calvin rebuffs all inquiry by the blunt announcement that the elect are known to God alone. The Romish Church insists that the true Church universal must, of necessity, be visible: the Reformers inclined to treat it as essentially invisible: while the Westminster sages refused to be impaled upon either horn of the dilemma, but boldly bestrode it, affirming that the Church universal is at the same

THE "HOLY CATHOLIC CHURCH"

time visible and invisible. As invisible, it "consists of the whole number of the elect, that have been, are, or shall be, gathered into one, under Christ the head thereof; and is the spouse, the body, the fulness of him that filleth all in all." As visible, it "consists of all those throughout the world that profess the true religion, together with their children." In this latter sense only is it affirmed to be "the kingdom of our Lord Jesus Christ, the house and family of God, out of which there is no ordinary possibility of salvation."

In this last sentence we reach a direct affirmation concerning our main subject of inquiry; but it plunges us into still further difficulty. Instead of one universal Church, as a subject of possible identification with the kingdom, we are furnished with two, whose constituency must be widely different. For the "elect," past, present and to come, are freely admitted not to be coincident in outline with the existing company of ostensible church-members and their indiscriminately registered households. But, unfortunately, the Church selected for identification with the kingdom is not that referred to by Paul, under the figurative terms, "the spouse," "the body," etc., but another and purely fictitious organization concerning which we shall consult Paul in vain, since he never in the remotest way alludes to it.

It is true that in the *Baptist* Confession of 1643 there appears the statement (Art. XXXIII.) that "Jesus Christ hath here on earth a spiritual kingdom, which is his church"; but that the compilers did not thereby intend a world-church as correspondent to a world-kingdom, is evident from the tenor of the whole article, which specifically refers to "a company of visible saints" united together "by mutual agreement," as well as from the character of the proof-texts cited, not one of which is included among the passages relied upon to substantiate the notion of a universal Church. In the Confession of 1689 the Westminster definition of the invisible "catholic or universal Church" is bodily appropriated, while the so-called visible catholic Church, there mentioned, is ignored, and the identity of either with the kingdom fails also to be asserted. Throughout the rest of the document reference is almost uniformly had to the local body. The single article

THE "HOLY CATHOLIC CHURCH"

alluded to must, therefore, be recognized as a fruit of the eager desire expressed, in their prefatory words, by the compilers, to avoid the suspicion of an "itch to clog religion with new words." They have, as they affirm, carried their conciliatory purpose so far as to "make use of the very same words with them both" (Presbyterians and Congregationalists), wherever harmony of general opinion would permit. While their adoption of so much of the Westminster formula is an unquestionable assent to the notion involved, it can not be regarded as so positive and well considered an indorsement as if the language had been wrought out on an independent Scriptural basis by themselves.

It will be noticed, furthermore, that this Confession of Faith was modestly claimed to be approximate only, and that our fathers declared they would "account him their chiefest friend that shall be an instrument to convert us from any error that is in our ways." The Westminster folk, whom they loyally followed in part, have already been convicted of an "error in their ways," as Dr. Candlish confesses, in their overconfident identification of the Church

THE CHURCH AND THE KINGDOM

and the kingdom. Having proven untrustworthy at one point, it can not be unlawful to suspect possible error and misleading influence at another. A hint of disposition to distrust at this point may possibly appear in the circumstance that the later New Hampshire Confession, probably more widely adopted than any other by the Baptist churches of America, excludes all reference whatever to a "universal Church," visible or invisible.

After this protracted and unfruitful reconnoitering of the exegetical horizon, we may be forgiven, at least, for the suspicion that infallible guides are not in sight. However uniform the interpreters may be in their agreement that there is a universal Church, they are as persistently uniform in **mutual contradiction as to its nature.**

II.

HISTORIC EMERGENCE OF THE MODERN IDEA OF A WORLD-CHURCH

1. *The churches of the early period.* It is commonly agreed among scholars that the "bishop" or "presbyter" of the New Testament was the pastor of a local church, and that there is no hint of the formal organization of these churches into diocesan or other unitary groups. By slow degrees, in sub-apostolic and later times, the pastor of the local body became the bishop of the city and then of the *paroikia* or group of neighboring cities. "In great cities," says Du Chesne, a Romanist writer (in "Christian Worship," p. 401, and speaking of the fourth century), there were many churches, but all "expansions of the cathedral, rather than distinct parishes." The sacred elements consecrated in this central "cathedral" were sent around to the branches in the city, and later sent to those in the larger diocese, and they were thus taught to regard themselves

THE CHURCH AND THE KINGDOM

as fractional parts of the diocesan whole.

2. *The World-Church under Constantine.* It was not until the calling of an "ecumenical council" by the world-ruler, Constantine, that the notion of an ecumenical church seems to have ripened into definite form, and the word "catholic" to have been introduced into the so-called Apostles' Creed. Councils had hitherto been local, advisory in character, independently summoned by local bodies, and composed of laity as well as clergy. But the Council of Nicea was officially summoned by the head of the Christian empire and composed of the official heads of all its component ecclesiastical and civic dioceses. Its decrees were endorsed by the imperial hand, and the church thus consolidated into a world organism. So came, later, the "Holy Roman Empire," and in the end the "Holy Catholic Church" of modern times, under a Christian Pontifex Maximus, as lineal successor of Peter and Constantine alike.

III.

APPEAL TO THE NEW TESTAMENT IN DEFENSE OF THE IDEA

I. PRELIMINARY CAUTION AS TO EXEGETIC BIAS.

1. *From ecclesiastical environment.* It must be borne in mind that, from the time of Constantine, the great body of New Testament interpreters have been themselves identified with an imperial, a national, a hereditary, or some other form of ecclesiastical organization which compelled them, if loyal, to find justification in the Scriptures of such larger organism than the local church. Consciously or unconsciously, the text of the New Testament has been in danger of being thus made a "nose of wax" through subtle ingenuity of exegesis in instinctive self-defense.

2. *From theoretic exigencies created by persistence in traditional practices.*

Dr. Hodge naively confesses, as we have seen, that "in order to justify the baptism

THE CHURCH AND THE KINGDOM

of infants, we must attain and authenticate such an idea of the church as that it shall include the children of believing parents." That is to say, that, having determined that infant baptism must, to use the Anglican phrase, "in anywise be retained in the church," it becomes necessary so to interpret the language of Scripture as to justify its retention.

In like manner Cardinal Newman frankly confesses that on finding certain practices of the Romish Church apparently at war with Scripture, naturally understood, he has invented a new meaning of the words, as a "hypothesis to escape a difficulty." All exegesis controlled by the purpose to reach a predetermined conclusion is thereby also predetermined to be arbitrary, if not willfully wrong in result. We have need to remind ourselves constantly of this tendency to partizan *strabismus* in reviewing the interpretations of others, and no less need to caution ourselves against falling into like error ourselves, since the temptation is one common to man. We can, at least, being conscious of the peril, strive the more earnestly to be candidly judicial in our inquiry.

II. Chief Premises Relied On.—All theorists who hold to the conception that the primary meaning of the word "church" in the New Testament is universal, rather than individual, rest upon the inference drawn from one, or both, of two closely allied assumptions. These are:

1. *That the Christian Church and the Kingdom of Heaven are identical.* If this assumption be correct, it follows, of course, that since the Kingdom is one and universal, the Church, its counterpart, must be the same. Whether the assumption is in fact justified by the teaching of the New Testament must remain to be later considered. Meantime, we may notice with what confidence the affirmation of identity is made, and glance at the circumstances which seem to have contributed to its acceptance as valid.

Meyrick, the writer of the article on the "church" in Smith's Bible Dictionary, settles the question thus categorically: "In Matt. 16: 18, it is *formally,* as elsewhere *virtually,* affirmed that the Kingdom of Heaven and the Church are identical." Cremer, in his "New Testament Lexicon," with equal absoluteness declares that the

THE CHURCH AND THE KINGDOM

"application of the word (*ekklesia*) to the Church universal is primary, and that to the individual church secondary, as is clear from the Old Testament (Septuagint) use of the word, and from the fundamental statement of Christ in Matt. 16: 18." In Carr's volume on "The Church and the Roman Empire" (one of the "Epochs of Church History" Series) the identity of the Church and the Kingdom is plainly s u p p o s e d throughout as indisputable:

"The direction given to the advance of Christianity was clearly ruled by the term which describes it—the *basileia*, the Kingdom, the *imperium* of God. For although the spiritual aspect of the Kingdom was carefully defined and pressed, yet this term adopted by the Master and always prominent in the teaching of his apostles could not be used without a sense of comparison with the Roman Empire. In inscriptions and in all contemporary historians, such as Zosimus, Socrates or Sozomen, the Roman emperor was known as *basileus*, and the Greek for empire was *basileia*. In 1 Tim. 2: 2 and in 1 Pet. 2: 17, the request (for prayer for 'kings') of course alludes to Claudius or Nero. . . .

THE "HOLY CATHOLIC CHURCH"

"This thought (of possible rivalry) . . . explains the attitude of the civil power toward the Church—there was a point where persecution became a necessity—and it explains the magnificent courage of the Christian martyrs, and the far-reaching hopes and exalted confidence of great churchmen in every age.

"The very words of the Lord's Prayer carried in them the seeds of a revolution. No Roman magistrate could hear with perfect complacency that the words 'Thy kingdom come' (*basileia*) were uttered in a most sacred, and in some sense a secret, form of prayer every day by hundreds of thousands who formed part of what seemed to him to be an organized and dangerous conspiracy. . . .

"It (the instinctive sense of danger) had already appeared in the trial of Christ before Pilate: 'If thou let this man go, thou art not Cæsar's friend' (John 19:12); and it appears in the trial of Paul before the politarchs of Thessalonica (Acts 17:7): 'These all act contrary to the decrees of Cæsar, saying that there is another king, one Jesus.' . . .

"In this way Cæsarism and Christianity

THE CHURCH AND THE KINGDOM

clashed. In this way the idea of the *basileia* worked itself out to the supremacy of the *Church* in the world. All that vast development which we lightly trace in these pages sprang from the thought which Jesus infused into this conception of a *basileia*. The possession of this imperial idea made *church* history what it was. . . .

"In this contest of rival powers, the two *basileiai* or *imperia* of Rome and the *Church*, which began their careers almost simultaneously, the *Church* won the victory. In a true sense, the 'kingdoms of the world' became 'the kingdom of Christ.'"

The origin of the idea in question, the identification of Church and Kingdom (or "empire," as it might properly have been rendered), thus seems to have been contemporaneous with the nominal Christianization of the Roman Empire. The earlier Christian writers know nothing apparently, as we have seen, of an actual world-church, and consequently nothing of its identity with the world-kingdom.

It is true that from the beginning there existed, among the Jews, the notion that Jesus, if he were the true Messiah, would set up an earthly kingdom. They tried to

THE "HOLY CATHOLIC CHURCH"

"take him by force, and make him king." And the notion lingered among his disciples to the last, notwithstanding his protests. For even after his resurrection his disciples expressed the hope that he would again "restore the kingdom to Israel." But the establishment of the kingdom expected by them involved the forcible overthrow of the Roman Empire and building on its ruins. The establishment of churches by preaching occupied their immediate attention. Preaching was a thing to be done by them. The kingdom, on the other hand, was a distinct thing, to be the outcome of the Lord's personal return and victorious assault upon the existing world-power.

Until the time of Constantine, therefore, the "kingdom of God" was regarded as the foe and appointed destroyer by force, of the "kingdom of Cæsar." But, with the conversion of Constantine, it dawned upon Eusebius and some of his contemporaries that the establishment of the Messianic reign, for which they had been waiting, was to be by the Christianization, and so by the absorption into itself, of the existing empire. Jewish as well as Gentile analogies suggested unification of earthly and heaven-

THE CHURCH AND THE KINGDOM

ly rule. For the Messianic King was to be a "priest upon his throne," and the Roman emperor was Pontifex Maximus as well as Imperator. The notions of universality of the "church" in world-range, and of its identity with the "kingdom" as a visible world-power, were thus twin-born. After this time only, the "holy church," of the Apostles' Creed became the "Holy *Catholic* Church." The church had been conceived of as the sphere of the bishop. This sphere, which was at first the local body, had gradually grown to comprehend dependent or affiliated bodies, until it had taken in a "diocese." Both Jewish and Gentile analogies now suggested the idea of a consolidated church-kingdom, of which the emperor should be the ecclesiastico-political head. The Jewish priestly organization had culminated in a high priest, as did the Roman in the Pontifex Maximus. The religious and the secular national life of the Romans were identical, as among the Jews; the priestly being, at the same time, a political office, controlled and paid by the state. The *jus publicum* was at the same time *jus sacrum*. Constantine was, by virtue of his imperial office, Pontifex Maximus of Rome. Why not also,

THE "HOLY CATHOLIC CHURCH"

by virtue of the same secular headship of a Christian empire, the Pontifex Maximus of an imperial church? The idea was distinctly broached in the calling of the first "Ecumenical Council," and the decrees of that body, enforced by the legislation of the empire, for the first time blended "church" and "kingdom" into one. After this, only, the phrase "Holy Catholic Church" appeared in the Apostles' Creed, and the "Holy Roman Empire" took historic form. In the latter, the strife of pope and emperor issued at last in the establishment of the pope as Universal Sovereign and Pontifex Maximus, the assumed heir, by right of succession both to Peter and Augustus, as the world's ecclesiastic and secular head. The notions of universality of the "church" in extent, and of its identity with the "kingdom" as a visible world-power, were thus twin-born. The notion of universality and visibility had finally become so closely interwoven, and both so indissolubly associated with the Roman establishment, that the Augsburg Confession—the first Protestant formula—wholly ignored the term *catholic* in defining the church, returning to the *earlier* form, "the holy church." Luther, in his catechism, satisfied himself with "the holy Christian church." It was not without reasonable justification, therefore, that Bossuet charged upon the Reformers the later invention of the notion of an "invisible catholic" church, as a device to preserve the idea of catholicity without its inevitable implication of external reality.

But we need not continue this preliminary inquiry further. It is plain that the demands of current imperial, national and hereditary ecclesiastical theory are of such a character as to make the retention of the notion of a Church universal necessary. It is plain that that notion has historically arisen in connection with the development of an actual ecclesiastical world-power. It is plain that this has always justified itself exegetically by confining itself solely to Jewish precedent, and to the Septuagint, in its search for a clue to the meaning of the word *ecclesia*. That this precommittal to a theory has exerted a certain strabismic pressure upon the exegetic eye may be independently inferred from the preposterous issue to which it has led. For it has compelled the absurd conclusion that the New Testament writers have almost uniformly

THE "HOLY CATHOLIC CHURCH"

used the word, without notice, in a non-natural and presumably unsuspected sense.

As an exquisite illustration of the ingenuity with which the language of Scripture may be manipulated to support a preconceived theory, and so to justify an existing institution, let us examine Dr. (afterward Cardinal) Newman's argument in three of his "Sermons on Subjects of the Day" (before referred to). In the first of these ("The Christian Church a Continuation of the Jewish") he contends from the words of Isaiah (37:31: "The remnant that is escaped from the house of Judah shall again take root downward and bear fruit upward") that the word "remnant," also emphasized elsewhere, implies an actual survival of the Jewish national organization without breach of continuity, passing over into the Christian Church.

In the second sermon ("The Principle of Continuity between the Jewish and Christian Churches") he builds upon Paul's language in Col. 2: 19-22, in which Christians are exhorted "to hold fast the Head," and warned against being entangled again by the "rudiments of the world," or subjecting themselves to "ordinances" fashioned after "the precepts and doctrines of men." As these words were addressed to quondam heathen, it is inferred that they were meant to refer to and condemn the substitution of human for divinely appointed rites. The further inference follows that the "forms, rites and polity" of the Christian Church are divinely predetermined by the authoritative temple service, which must be taken as an inviolable "pattern."

In the third sermon ("The Christian Church an Imperial Power") the argument culminates in the claim that the fulfillment of prophecy requires the emergence into visibility of the Church as a world-power. Isaiah (2:2: "It shall come to pass in the last days that the mountain of the Lord's house shall be established in the top of the mountain, and shall be exalted above the hills, and all nations shall flow unto it") is claimed to have foretold a local center of visible national aggregation and universal authority. That a literal world-dominion is expected to be established at this center, the words of Daniel are said to make indisputable. For he puts the "kingdom" which the "God of heaven" is to set up (Dan. 2:44) over against the distinctly identified

THE "HOLY CATHOLIC CHURCH"

e a r t h l y kingdoms previously mentioned. That the "kingdom of heaven," referred to in the New Testament, is identical with that referred to in prophecy, and that it is classed among visible earthly powers, is further confirmed by the circumstance that our Lord chooses (Matt. 13: 32) precisely the same symbol to describe it (a tree, in whose branches the fowl take refuge) which had been employed by Ezekiel (17: 23) when referring to the coming heavenly Kingdom, and also (31: 6) when pointing to the Assyrian Empire. Jeremiah's promise that David shall never want a man to sit upon the throne of the house of Israel" (33: 17), often repeated by Ezekiel and other prophets (Ezekiel declaring that David *himself* shall be "their prince forever"—37: 25), falls into line in support of the theory that the "Kingdom of heaven," otherwise called the "Christian Church," has been prophetically designated as a visible imperial world-power.

The application of this argument is quick and inevitable. The *basileia* which Christ transfers to Peter (Matt. 16: 19) is not spoken of as yet to be inaugurated; for it is the already long-established kingdom of Israel, of which as heir and successor of

THE CHURCH AND THE KINGDOM

David he is the rightful possessor and donor.

The parallel reference to an *ecclesia* yet to be built on Peter naturally follows upon the allusion to "keys"; suggesting at once the familiar "key of the house of David," and leading on to the still more familiar Septuagint notion of *ecclesia* as describing the "house of Israel." If it be true that the *ecclesia* now referred to is in some sense a new structure, this is only because the "tabernacle of David" is conceived of, from one point of view, as having "fallen down" and is now to be rebuilt in accordance with the express promise of prophecy (Amos 9: 11). The apostle James so understands it, as reported in Acts 16: 15.

By such exegetical manœuvres, unrivaled in astuteness, the Scripture has been made to buttress the blasphemous assumptions of the Papacy. The Church of Rome becomes thus the very "kingdom" which the "God of heaven" was to set up, out-topping all other earthly kingdoms; and such a miscreant, for instance, as Alexander Borgia, a perjurer, libertine, an assassin, becomes the heir and fulfiller of Messianic prophecy, and the divinely accredited "prince of the kings of the earth." When our Lord declares, ere he

THE "HOLY CATHOLIC CHURCH"

leaves the earth, that "all power is given to him in heaven and in earth," it is only that He may indicate the plenitude of power of which Peter and his successors are to become the residuary legatees, custodians, and vehicle. Henceforth the Petrine throne becomes the visible counterpart of the "great white throne" in heaven, precisely as the seat of the imperial Cæsar answers to that of the Capitoline Jove. So that it is no more illegitimate for a Pope to speak of himself as *"alter deus"* or as "filling the place of the true God on earth," than for a successor of Augustus to call himself *"Divus* Cæsar." Invested with the triple crown of dominion over heaven, earth, and hell, and bearing the "two swords" of civic and ecclesiastic mastery, the sole "vicegerent of God on earth" may well laugh at the rival or independent claims of every other church or kingdom.

How, then, does the Anglican theory differ from that of Rome, and on what modification in exegetical procedure does it rest? The answer may be prognosticated from the circumstances which attended and controlled the organization of the Church of England as an independent body. When Henry

THE CHURCH AND THE KINGDOM

VIII. abruptly cut the hawser which held his kingdom in tow of the Papacy, it went apart on its new voyage with its whole cargo of ritual, tradition, and ecclesiastico-civic polity theoretically unbroken. But a national church could no longer invidiously claim for itself an exclusive world-embracing jurisdiction. Instead of a single imperial headship, consequently, it became necessary to establish a multiple headship of the church, under the joint dominion of all Christian kings. This did not necessitate the abandonment of the traditional notion of literal continuity from the Jewish original. It was necessary only to substitute the *college* of Apostles, as Canon Fremantle luminously explains, for *Peter* alone. Were they not to "sit on twelve thrones judging the twelve tribes of Israel"; and what could these "tribes" be if not the nations of Christendom, which make up at once the "Kingdom of Heaven," and the "Holy Catholic Church"? There is in England, as Canon Fremantle further affirms, no such thing as an "established church" (meaning thereby a worshiping body), but only an "established clergy." The nation *is* the church, the apostolic succession in which attaches

THE "HOLY CATHOLIC CHURCH"

primarily to the sovereign as head, and only subordinately to prelates charged with supervision of its territorial segments. Hooker, accordingly, correctly affirmed that "there is not a man of the Church of England but the same man is a member of the commonwealth, nor any member of the commonwealth which is not also of the Church of England." And Hobbes, in his "Leviathan," rightly also maintained that, as God's accredited spokesman, the king had the power to establish an ultimate standard of right by his decree. Canon Curteis, in his Bampton Lectures, reasoning from the same premises, condemns as derelict any priest who allows a babe born within the limits of his bailiwick to remain unbaptized, no matter what may be the views or wishes of its parents. The word "bailiwick" is used advisedly; for the English "parish" is the civic as well as ecclesiastical unit of territorial partition for administrative purposes, and the local priest is as truly a civic official invested with power to enforce his claims therein as the sheriff. A recent writer of the same church (Winterbotham: "Kingdom of Heaven"), identifying kingdom and church after the traditional fashion, falls into this curious strain of inferential comment; viz.:

"It is clear that the baptism of infants stands or falls with the parable of the drag-net, and the saying, 'Of such is the Kingdom of Heaven.' Babies, as such, *can* only have to do with the kingdom so far as it is a net, including all within a certain area, without choice on their part, without moral discrimination on the part of the net." Bishop Moorhouse, of Manchester, in like manner, deprecates church discipline, on the basis of the parable of the tares, from which he derives the cautionary hint that exclusion may prevent the intrusive tares from being "converted into wheat."

The Anglican theory, then, is evidently a vigorous shoot from the old Romish stock of theoretic Jewish continuity, slightly variant in contour only because of a new exegetic element contributed by a different soil of circumstance.

Dr. Candlish (a Presbyterian, and therefore confronted by the express statement of the Westminster Confession that the "visible Church, which is also catholic and universal under the gospel, . . . *is* the Kingdom of our Lord Jesus Christ"), in his lectures

THE "HOLY CATHOLIC CHURCH"

on the "Kingdom of God" (1884), raises the question of identity thus:

"Is the notion of the Kingdom of God really different from that of the Church of Christ? Are not these just different names for the same thing? So it has often been assumed, and the terms have been used as synonyms, and discussions about the Kingdom of God or of Christ have often passed on, without explanation or argument for their identity, to conclusions about the Church. This has been very generally done, though in many different ways, *from the time of Augustine* until quite recently. Of late, however, the notions of the Church and the Kingdom have not only been distinguished, but, by some, entirely separated from each other; and it has been held to be of great doctrinal importance to maintain the distinction." He thereupon proceeds at some length to prove that the two are "not identical, as was assumed in former times." He cites many modern authorities as maintaining the distinction; such as Baumgarten, Auberlen, Delitzsch, Kurtz, Hoffman, Meyer, etc. (Fairbairn, a Congregationalist, defends the distinction earnestly in his "Studies in the Life of Christ," 111.)

THE CHURCH AND THE KINGDOM

But, while repudiating the unwarranted assumption of identity, Dr. Candlish accepts, without protest, a prior assumption which is equally arbitrary, without which the erroneous identification pointed out would have been impossible. For, of course, the notion of equivalence with a confessedly world-wide kingdom could not attach to a church which was not also reckoned world-wide. He takes it for granted, therefore, that the word "church" in the New Testament refers, presumptively, at least in all cases where the context does not forbid, to the "Church universal," and that this is its prevalent and normal sense.

But it ought to have occurred to him that this proposition needs proof as urgently as the one whose overhasty acceptance he has condemned. For the term "universal" is not explicitly applied to the Church by any New Testament writer; there is no hint in any reference to a local church that it is part of any such body; and the idea of universality is distinctly excluded, as Dr. Candlish himself admits, in an overwhelming majority of instances. Dr. Hort, in a recently published critical study of the subject in his "New Testament Ecclesia," concludes

THE "HOLY CATHOLIC CHURCH"

that the word nowhere suggests a broader reference than to the local body (aside from our Lord's allusion in Matt. 16: 18), except in the brief Epistles to the Ephesians and Colossians. Dr. Candlish goes even further in conceding that the broader meaning is not to be found in the Gospels, but in the two Epistles named alone. The word occurs but thirteen times in these Epistles, the local limitation being explicit in two of these at least. There remain, then, less than a dozen, out of considerably more than a hundred instances of its occurrence, in which the universal sense is claimed even possibly to be the fit one. To attempt to settle the proper meaning of a word upon the authority of a doubtful ten per cent., as against that of an explicit ninety per cent. of actual usage, is surely a headlong procedure.

Modern scholarship strongly inclines, as we have seen, to treat the traditional identification of the "church" and the "kingdom" as erroneous. It proposes a return to the text of the New Testament to determine exegetically "in what way these terms are related to each other." This is tantamount to an admission that scholars have erred as to the normal meaning of one or the other

THE CHURCH AND THE KINGDOM

of the words involved (*basileia* and *ecclesia*). But the confusing error can not have arisen in connection with the former of these two words: there is no dispute as to the characteristics or universality of the "kingdom." Nor could it arise in connection with the latter, when understood in the local sense indisputably fastened upon it in the majority of the cases in which it occurs: for in this sense it is clearly not coextensive with the former. It is only when the additional sense of universality is attached to *ecclesia*, and this sense is made primary, that the possibility of confusion begins. It is at this point, therefore, that caution is especially necessary in attempting an independent inquiry as to the intended force of the words in the New Testament.

It is plain, then, that the conception of the New Testament Church as universal in extent, in so far as it is based upon the identity of Church and Kingdom, can not be traced further back than the so-called Ecumenical Council of Nicea and the assumed consolidation of church and empire under Constantine. But there remains another conception supposed to justify the conception of the Church as a unit, world-wide in range. It is

THE "HOLY CATHOLIC CHURCH"

2. *That the Christian Church is a literal prolongation of the Israelitish.* Sayford, in Hastings' Bible Dictionary, under the title "Church," summarizes the Scriptural data on which this theory rests, as follows:

There was "a church within the Jewish nation to which Paul alludes as the 'Israel of God' (Gal. 6:16). It is singled out from the nation by Paul's words, 'Not *all* they which are of Israel are Israel' (implying that *some* of them are—Rom. 9:6): these are the 'remnant according to the election of grace' 'in this present time' (Rom. 11: 16-24)."

To the same effect says Dr. Chas. Hodge ("Church Polity," 59-67): "The Protestant distinction between the Church visible and invisible, nominal and real, is that which Paul makes between 'Israel after the flesh' and 'Israel after the Spirit.' . . . It is to be remembered that there were two covenants with Abraham. By the one, his natural descendants through Isaac were constituted a commonwealth, an external, visible community. By the other his spiritual descendants were constituted a church. The parties to the former covenant were God and the nation; to the other, God and his true people.

THE CHURCH AND THE KINGDOM

... When Christ came, 'the commonwealth' was abolished, and there was nothing put in its place. The church remained. There was no external covenant, nor promises of external blessing on condition of external rites and subjection. There was a spiritual society with spiritual promises, on the condition of faith in Christ. ... The church is, therefore, in its essential nature, a body of believers, and not an external society, requiring merely external profession as the condition of membership."

But this definition, being of the invisible Church, is necessarily applicable only to the ideal and not the actual body. It must be supplemented, or rather replaced, accordingly, by Dr. Hodge's own definition of the visible or actual Church—the New Testament church which we are seeking ("Syst. Theol.," III., 547-558):

"1. The invisible church is a divine institution.

"2. The visible church does not consist exclusively of the regenerate. Our Lord compares his external kingdom, or visible church, to a field in which tares and wheat grow together.

THE "HOLY CATHOLIC CHURCH"

"3. The commonwealth of Israel was the church.

"4. The church under the new dispensation continues identical with that under the old."

It is obvious that this, and not the other definition, must be resorted to, as he himself immediately adds, to "authenticate such an idea of the church as that it shall include the children of believing parents." Now, the invisible Church is not an "institution" at all. The only institution bearing that name is, therefore, continuous with the Old Testament institution, the Israelitish church, or Abrahamic race. Cremer, accordingly, bases his claim that the primary meaning of the word is universal, chiefly on the fact that *ekklesia* in the LXX. (*qahal* in the Hebrew) designated the "people of Israel collectively," and that in the New Testament it must correspondingly refer to the people of God collectively, since they constitute the new Israel.

I may remark, in passing, that the distinguished textual critic and exegete, Dr. Hort—to whose book on the subject reference has been and will be later made—entirely repudiates this rendition of the word

THE CHURCH AND THE KINGDOM

qahal and its Greek synonym *ekklesia.* The Hebrew word, he says, "is derived from an obsolete root, meaning to call or summon, and its resemblance to the Greek *kaleo* naturally suggested to the Septuagint translators the word *ekklesia,* derived from *kaleo* (rather than *ekkaleo*) in precisely the same sense. . . . There is no foundation for the widely spread notion that *ekklesia* means a people or a number of individual men called out of the world of mankind. . . . The original calling out is simply the calling of the citizens of a Greek town out of their houses, by the herald's trumpet, to summon them to the assembly; and Num. 10: 1-7 shows that the summons to the Jewish assembly was made in the same way ('Make thee two trumpets of silver . . . and thou shalt use them for the calling of the congregation,' etc.). So that the term, in either language, referred to a local assembly only."

It will be observed that the Roman Catholic theory also maintains like continuity of the Christian with the Israelitish church. Cardinal Newman entitles one of his sermons, as we have seen, "The Christian Church a Continuation of the Jewish." But while the Calvinistic theorist finds the line

THE "HOLY CATHOLIC CHURCH"

of continuity in the Abrahamic covenant and race lineage, the Romanist emphasizes rather the Davidic, with its promises of perpetual royal succession.

The reflex influence of circumstance upon exegesis is especially conspicuous when we come to Calvin and the *Presbyterian* bodies that sprang from his teaching. Having determined that infant baptism must "in any wise be retained in the church," but being also irrevocably committed to the doctrine of justification by faith alone, Calvin was obliged to forego the traditional defense of infant baptism on the basis of baptismal regeneration, and to abandon the passage in which that doctrine had confidently entrenched itself (John 3:5). Deprived of this stronghold, he could find no refuge to fall back upon except the Abrahamic covenant, which, if accepted as literally perennial, would take in the children of the direct stock, and also all the offspring of members of the household who had been "bought with money" (as the General Assembly was obliged to decide when the matter was brought up in this country). But as "every man that is circumcised is a debtor to do the whole law," according to Paul, it would appear that Calvin, having allowed his wheel to be caught by a single point in the rut of Jewish continuity, was unable to extricate himself from its entire and despotic mastery. A revived Jewish theocracy, therefore, emerged into form in Geneva, which assumed to blend the civic and religious at every point, regulating the diet and bedtime of the citizens, delivering the disobedient child over to the "secular arm" for punishment, and purging Servetus of heresy by fire. Although bitterly opposed to prelatic despotism, Calvin found in the "elders of Israel" a precedent for the establishment of a body of "ruling elders" who, in the person of the aristocracy of Geneva, the Huguenot leaders of high blood in France, and the "lords of the congregation" in Scotland, took over to a lay syndicate all the centralized power before vested in pope or king. The theocracy of New England, the normal outgrowth of the Calvinistic scheme, was justly satirized by one of its victims long after as a transfer of tyranny from the "lord bishops" to the "lord brethren." It is obviously necessary, under this theory, to maintain the literal identity of the Christian Church as a national body, with the Israelitish organiza-

THE "HOLY CATHOLIC CHURCH"

tion. Presbyterian writers on the subject, with almost unbroken uniformity, begin their history of the Christian Church with an account of the commonwealth of Israel; proceeding without recognized gap to treat the events that followed Pentecost as only a new phase of an old thing. That Stephen in his address (Acts 7: 38) speaks of a "church in the wilderness" is seized upon, sometimes, as conclusive in the premises. Dr. Hodge, in his discussions, does not scruple to say explicitly that "the Church under the new dispensation is identical with that under the old."

All theories holding to a literal Church universal thus turn back to the Old Testament to justify that conception. In Cardinal Newman's sermon above referred to, only two out of twenty-five Scriptural citations made are from the New Testament.

It remains, now, to examine the New Testament itself to find in how far this assumption of dependence on the Old Testament is justified. It is worth while to inquire whether the distinctively Christian Church had appeared before Christ, its supposed founder, and to judge from his own language and that of his authorized spokesmen, the Apostles, what was their notion of it as indicated in their recorded words.

This inquiry ought, as far as is practicable, to be purely and impartially exegetic in character. To such an inquiry let us next turn.

PART V.
THE CHURCH OF THE NEW TESTAMENT

I.

THE WORD "ECCLESIA" IN THE NEW TESTAMENT

I. INVERSE METHOD.—Meyrick (Smith's Bible Dictionary, 1893, *s. v.* "Church") remarks concerning the word *ekklesia* that the "ordinary classical meaning of the word (assembly called out by magistrate or by legitimate authority) throws no light on the nature of the institution so designated in the New Testament," etc.

For up to about that time it had been generally held that the "New Testament Greek" was so thoroughly Hebraized, or otherwise arbitrarily remodeled by the Evangelists and Apostles, as to make it virtually an independent speech, requiring a special dictionary and grammar. Differing, as it plainly did, in verbal and syntactical form from the classical, it was assumed that secular literature or usage could not contribute to its understanding. Reference was, therefore, had to the Septuagint use of the word

THE CHURCH AND THE KINGDOM

ekklesia, and beyond that to the Hebrew word *qahal,* which it sometimes translated. It was, thereupon, inversely and most illogically inferred that, since *qahal* sometimes means the whole Israelitish people and is sometimes translated by *ekklesia,* therefore *ekklesia* must always take on like breadth of meaning. Reference to the LXX., however, will show that the Greek translators of the Old Testament, so far from encouraging such an implication, have carefully precluded it. For when *qahal* has the broad sense it is never translated by *ekklesia,* but by another Greek word.

The reflex method of interpretation is hazardous and treacherous, at the best. In Cardinal Manning's "Essays" may be found a defense of the Romish doctrine of transubstantiation, based on the statement that in the LXX. *trapeza* is sometimes employed to designate an altar. Therefore, it is argued, the table (*trapeza*) at which our Lord and his disciples were sitting at the institution of the last Supper must be counted an altar, and the Supper itself a sacrifice. By a similar indirect process of reasoning, Dr. Edward Beecher reached the conclusion that since there arose a dispute among John

Baptist's disciples "about purifying," baptism must have referred to purification, rather than regeneration, as its central idea—and must thereupon be properly symbolized by washing rather than immersion.

The scholastic philosophers in Galileo's day were content to argue that since God makes all things perfect, and the circle is the perfect form, it follows that the heavenly bodies must move in circles. Galileo thought it wiser to look through his telescope and discover directly how they do move. It seems better for us, also, instead of "fetching a compass" upon this Greek word, in order to learn its real meaning, to ascertain, if we can, by help of like direct methods, what idea the word in question was intended by the writer to convey, and what idea it did actually convey to those addressed. This brings us to ask for

II. THE NATURAL METHOD.—In Dr. J. H. Moulton's "Prolegomena" to his grammar of New Testament Greek, he begins with the remark that "as recently as 1895, in the beginning chapter of a beginner's manual of New Testament Greek," he had "defined the language as Hebraic Greek, colloquial Greek and late Greek. . . . In the *second* edition, issued in 1904, 'common Greek' is substituted for the first element in the definition. The disappearance of that word 'Hebraic' from its prominent place in our definition of New Testament language marks a change in our conceptions of the subject nothing less than revolutionary" (p. 1). This "Judaic" or "Biblical" Greek was supposed to be "found in the sacred writings" alone, "and never profaned by common use"; it was reckoned, to use Cremer's phrase, as the isolated "language of the Holy Ghost."

But the researches of Deissmann in 1895, and others since, have brought to light a great mass of Egyptian papyri and inscriptions which conclusively show "that hundreds of words, hitherto assumed to be 'Biblical'—technical words, as it were, called into existence or minted afresh by the language of Jewish religion—were in reality normal, first-century, spoken Greek. . . . The Holy Ghost spoke absolutely in the language of the common people, as we might surely have expected that he would . . . the very grammar and dictionary cry out against men who would allow the Scriptures to appear in

THE CHURCH OF THE NEW TESTAMENT

any other form than that 'understanded of the people'" (pp. 4, 5).

He adds that the Greek language was, in the first century, uncommonly uniform; that "it covered a far larger proportion of the civilized world than even English does today" (p. 5); that it "was the only period when a single language was understood throughout the countries which counted for the history of the empire"—a circumstance which he, as an "old-fashioned" person, "ventures to reckon Providential" (p. 6). He thinks it certain that there were few, if any, of those who heard Paul speaking from the stairs of Antonia in Jerusalem "who could not understand the world-language, or even speak it when necessary"; and what was true of the Jerusalem crowd he thinks would be even more absolutely true of the people of Galilee or Perea (p. 8). He cites Professor Mahaffy, the renowned Greek expert ("Hellenism in Alexander's Empire," 139 ff.), who holds that while "among his intimates our Lord spoke Aramaic . . . yet his public teaching, his discussions with the Pharisees, his talk with Pontius Pilate, were certainly carried on in Greek." From this extreme statement as to the uniform Greek

THE CHURCH AND THE KINGDOM

character of Christ's public utterance, Dr. Moulton differs; yet he adds that "he takes the direction in which every student of Hellenism is driven." As to Paul, Dr. Moulton concludes that "he had probably used Greek from childhood with entire freedom, and during the main part of his life may have had few opportunities of using Aramaic at all." "Finally," he adds, "we have the Gentile Luke and the *auctor ad Hebræos,* both of whom may well have known no Aramaic at all" (p. 10).

He sums up the discussion in these words: "What we can assert with assurance is that the papyri have finally destroyed the figment of a New Testament Greek which differed from that spoken by ordinary people in daily life throughout the Roman world" (p. 18).

But enough of citation on this head. I have given the latest impressions of competent scholars, based not on conjecture, but newly observed facts. They justify us in resorting confidently to common secular usage, rather than the remote Hebrew text or even the LXX., as the ultimate standard of interpretation of New Testament words; for even the LXX. must have referred to

THE CHURCH OF THE NEW TESTAMENT

such usage in the day of its translation. As that translation was made *long before* the New Testament era and the Greek *ecclesia* had existed as an institution long before the LXX., it will be safe to refer to the classical as well as contemporaneous or later authorities to learn the continuous and unchanging significance of the words used.

Before a more detailed study of the word *ekklesia* in its contextual relations, it may be well to look more broadly at the employment of the word in the New Testament, to learn whether the general principle of interpretation thus reached is fairly to be trusted in this specific case. Whether the word in question, that is to say, was used in its ordinary popular sense, or in a more restricted or artificial sense, may depend upon the question by whom, in addressing whom, and where the word was written. Let us, then, examine these particulars to learn

III. THE CIRCUMSTANTIAL PRESUMPTIONS OF THE CASE.

1. *Local occurrence of the word.* The word occurs 113 times in the New Testament. Nowhere in the Gospels, except in Matthew's record, and then only on two occasions. In the Acts, twenty-three times;

THE CHURCH AND THE KINGDOM

in the Epistles of Paul, sixty-one times; in the Epistle to the Hebrews, twice; in the Epistle of James, once; in the third Epistle of John and in the Revelation, twenty-one times. It is not found at all in Mark, Peter or Jude.

2. *Influences affecting writer or speaker.* Our Lord and all his Apostles were citizens of Galilee—familiarly known as "Galilee of the Gentiles." Matthew, who alone ascribes the word in question to him, was a publican, a Roman official, and therefore almost inevitably compelled to acquaintance with Greek. But, setting aside the Gospel allusion (which will be fully examined on its own merits later), it is noteworthy that the word is found almost exclusively in the writings of men of Gentile nativity or environment. The word does not occur at all in the Epistle of Peter. (The word "church" in 1 Pet. 5:13 is not in the original, and has been expunged from the translation by the revisers.) We are confined in our inquiry, then, almost exclusively to the writings of Paul, Luke and John. Of these, the first was brought up in the Gentile atmosphere of Tarsus, the second was himself of Gentile birth and training, and the third (who uses

THE CHURCH OF THE NEW TESTAMENT

the word twice in his third Epistle—vs. 6, 9 —and often—invariably in the plural—in the Apocalypse) was, at the time of writing, a citizen of the Greek community of Ephesus.

3. *Surroundings of persons addressed.* The Apostles, to whom our Lord spoke when using the word, were all Galileans. Theophilus, to whom Luke addressed the Book of Acts, was clearly a Gentile, and perhaps a Greek.

A hint may be derived, also, from a study of the relative use of the word *ekklesia* by the several epistolary writers. It occurs but rarely in letters directed to churches of Jewish proclivity. In the Epistle of James, for instance, it appears but once (5: 14); and is apparently used as a synonym of *synagogue,* earlier employed in the same Epistle (2: 2). In Hebrews, again, it presents itself only once; and there in connection with *paneguris* (12: 23). This added word carries with it an exceptional qualification of meaning which, taken with the context, transfers the whole subject of discussion into the heavenly world, beyond death, and so out of the region of earthly history and our present inquiry. (This is the conclusion of Thayer in his "New Testament Dictionary," of Sayford in the new Hastings' Bible Dictionary, and of other eminent Biblical scholars; and it affords the only satisfactory interpretation of the passage.)

It was to the Gentile church at Ephesus, and to those of neighboring Greek cities, that the Apocalypse was itself addressed. All Paul's writings, with the single exception of the Epistle to the Romans, were addressed to people resident in Greece proper, in Macedonia (which was also Greek), or in Asia Minor, where Greek institutions, speech and ideas were everywhere predominant. (Even as to Rome, Greek was so generally used that, according to Dr. Moulton, "a man need to have known little Latin to live in Rome itself.") It is particularly worthy of notice that in the only two Epistles where there is any tangible foothold for the broader interpretation of the word in question (according to the latest authorities), peculiar emphasis is laid upon the Gentile character of the persons addressed (Eph. 2: 11; 3: 1; 4: 17; Col. 1: 27; 2: 13; 4: 11, 12). The word to be interpreted appears then to have been almost always addressed, in the New Testament, in a Gentile language by Gentiles or Gentilized Jews to Gentiles. If there be any validity

THE CHURCH OF THE NEW TESTAMENT

whatever in the historico-grammatic theory of interpretation, the first step toward an authoritative apprehension of the idea intended to be conveyed, under such circumstances, would be an inquiry as to the possible existence of an established and familiar meaning of the word among a Gentile constituency. It can not reasonably be assumed that a Greek-speaking Jew, and particularly that such an intelligently self-adjusting writer as Paul, would stupidly or perversely employ a familiar word in a wholly foreign and unsuspected sense, borrowing such an extraordinary meaning from the Septuagint, of which they could not reasonably be presumed even to have heard.

In the cities of Greece, Macedonia and Asia Minor, Greek institutions and ideas prevailed; so that the people were familiar with the *ekklesia* itself as a concrete thing well known by name.

We may therefore proceed to inquire as to the meaning of the word in vernacular Greek, with the assurance that this was the meaning intended to be conveyed by it in the New Testament.

II.

THE GREEK "ECCLESIA"

I. A CHARACTERISTIC INSTITUTION.—
The Greeks differed radically from the Romans in their individualistic tendency. The "topography of the country," as Grote remarks in his "History" (II., 301), "fostered that powerful principle of repulsion which disposed even the smallest township to count itself a political unit apart from the rest, and to resist all ideas of coalescence, amicable or compulsory." Every city, accordingly, became an independent state. Aristotle, in his last work, made an analysis of 158 differing constitutions of such independent municipalities; for they were so jealous of their separate self-government that no one of them would accept the precedent set by another city, lest they should somehow jeopardize their liberty. They were as vigorously set upon individual independence as upon local self-government. They became, in the strictest sense, democratic—govern-

THE CHURCH OF THE NEW TESTAMENT

ments "of the people, for the people, by the people." Their courts as well as their legislative bodies were popular assemblies. Now, the summary form in which this pervading temper found most unique expression was the *ekklesia*. It was the organized assembly of the authorized voters of the local community met to transact business of common concern. It corresponded to the town-meeting of New England of later days. Even after the subjugation of Greece by the Romans, in the second century before the Christian era, the Greek cities retained nominal self-government. There remained in each an *ekklesia,* as its conspicuously central feature, at the time the New Testament was written.

Reference to the speeches of Demosthenes, the history of Thucydides, the comedies of Aristophanes, or other classical documents, will show how familiar and how uniform was the meaning of the word. Aristotle, in his "Politics," emphasizes the characteristics of the institution, as local and democratic, when he says that it is essential to the very nature of the city-state, of which it is the representative, that it should be small enough for all the citizens to know each other. Passing this limit, he says, it ceases to be properly a state, with a proper *ekklesia*. As a ship, only a span long on the one hand, or a quarter of a mile long on the other, has ceased to serve its appointed end, and so to be a ship at all, so an *ekklesia*, the extent of whose constituency forbids the normal interchange of opinion and discussion, ceases to be equal to its purpose, and therefore to be a proper *ekklesia* at all. The language of this authoritative exponent of Greek ideas has its obvious bearing on the question whether the term *ekklesia* can ever be extended to cover a world-body, or a body governed otherwise than democratically.

It may properly be added that the word *ekklesia* seems after Aristotle's day to have been sometimes still more restrictively understood, bringing it into still closer parallelism with New Testament usage. For Dr. Hatch, in his "Organization of the Early Churches," cites, from lately recovered inscriptions, frequent instances in which it is applied to local self-governing secular clubs or associations. In these the titles given some of the officers are identical with those of officers of New Testament churches.

II. RELATION OF "EKKLESIA" AND "BA-

SILEIA."—It will readily be inferred, from what has just been said, that the word *ekklesia* would call up, in the mind of an ordinary Greek, or Greek-speaking person, a conception not only not identical with, but in every particular the antithesis of, that suggested by the word *basileia*. The early Greek *basileus,* who had been an absolute local or tribal ruler, had long since vanished, as Aristotle explains in his "Politics." The title was now restricted exclusively to the head of the Roman Empire—the one sole master of the "habitable world." The word *basileia* had, therefore, come to carry with it the inevitably associated notion of world range and mastery. Our Lord's allusion to a new *basileia* (which might have been with even greater fitness translated "empire" rather than "kingdom" of God or of heaven) must suggest instantly and logically the idea of rivalry with Cæsar, and not of local insurrection or insubordination only; for two world-empires could not exist together (Acts 17: 7). Instances have already been cited from Carr, showing how instinctive was this sense of antagonism. Add to these the reply of the chief priests to Pilate's question, "Shall I crucify your king?" They promptly an-

THE CHURCH AND THE KINGDOM

swered, "We have no king but Cæsar" (John 19: 15). Note, also, the nature of the charge made against Jesus in Luke 23: 2: "We found this man perverting our nation, and forbidding to give tribute to Cæsar, and saying that he himself is Christ, a king." This inevitable suggestion of clashing jurisdictions explains, also, the "craftiness" of the chief priests, noticed by Luke in connection with the incident (recorded also by Matthew and Mark) in which they demanded of our Lord whether it was lawful to "give tribute to Cæsar." For had the word *basileia*, used by him as describing the new *regime* to be set up, meant to the ordinary hearer only a local and subordinate *regime*, its threatened establishment would have been insubordination only—a less serious offense. But if the broader meaning necessarily attached to the word, he could not escape the charge afterward actually made of attempted world-rivalry with Cæsar.

But over against this single, comprehensive, world-extensive conception, the word *ekklesia* set up an idea as distinctly local, partitive and multiple. The empire was, and must be, one. But there might be as many *ekklesiai* as there were Greek cities. Even

THE CHURCH OF THE NEW TESTAMENT

the Latin cities had their local *comitia,* which the eminent historian Freeman declares to have been the exact equivalent of the Greek *ekklesia,* each being the counterpart of the later Saxon town-meeting. The *basileia* was centered in the *basileus,* as its etymological form indicates, and was therefore necessarily monocratic: the *ekklesia,* from like etymological implication, must derive its central significance from the whole body of people assembled, and be democratic. The autonomy of the gathered group, as contrasted with individual lordship over it, was essential to the conception of the thing itself.

Since the two words in question must have suggested to the ordinary Greek mind notions directly and irreconcilably antithetic, it does not seem strange that modern scholars have begun to hesitate before counting them as being identical in force in New Testament usage. Dr. A. M. Fairbairn (in his "Studies in the Life of Christ"), after pointing out the grounds of such irreconcilability, concludes that "the church and the kingdom may thus more properly be contrasted than compared. . . . The church was to promote the ends, realize the ideals, of the kingdom. If *basileia* was steeped in Hebrew, *ekklesia* was penetrated with Greek, associations." This last remark is significant in connection with the circumstance that, in the new dispensation, the Greek language, with its existing fixedness of meaning, was providentially chosen as the medium of revelation, rather than the equally fixed, but then practically dead, Hebrew.

III. BEARING OF THE SEPTUAGINT ON NEW TESTAMENT USAGE OF "EKKLESIA."—Dr. B. H. Carroll, of Baylor University, a very thorough scholar, has collated all instances of the occurrence of *ekklesia* in the LXX. He finds them to be ninety-two in number. Not a single one of these has a broader meaning than that thus far assigned to it as familiar to the common Greek citizen. As confirming this statement, he gives the translation of the word in our Revised Version, it being there uniformly rendered "assembly" or "congregation."

It has been affirmed, however, that the word "congregation," here used as the equivalent of *ekklesia*, and the word *qahal*, which it translates in the passages in question, refers to the whole nation; and that the word *ekklesia*, thus broadened in meaning, has led to like broadening of meaning in its usage

THE CHURCH OF THE NEW TESTAMENT

by New Testament writers. Aside from the grotesque incongruity of the notion of an *unassembled* assembly or *uncongregated* congregation, we may wisely listen to the conclusions of the eminent linguistic master, Dr. F. J. A. Hort. "There are two words in Hebrew," he says, "referring to the Israelitish community. The one (*edhah*) designates the society itself, formed by the children of Israel or their representative heads, whether *assembled or not assembled.*" The other (*qahal*) is "properly their *actual meeting together.*" The two words sometimes occur together and may be rendered, in such a case, the "assembly of the congregation." The LXX. choice of the word *ekklesia* to designate the actual local assembly, rather than the Israelitish people at large, he thinks due, as before explained, to the apparent etymological origin of the Greek and Hebrew word from a common root, signifying to summon or call out.

In considering the possibility that the original Hebrew word, alleged to be of broader meaning, may have indirectly attached like breadth to the Greek in the New Testament writings, it may be observed that even were such a broader meaning trace-

THE CHURCH AND THE KINGDOM

able, which, as we have just seen, is denied by Hort, it seems incredible that it could have had the effect indicated. The Gentile communities, who were addressed, knew the word *ekklesia* well, whether heard in common speech or found in the LXX., and were not likely to attach gratuitously divergent meanings to it, wherever found. The supposed modification of meaning hidden in the Hebrew original could not have affected them, for they did not know Hebrew. Paul was most painstaking and most skillful in adjusting his forms of speech, so as to make himself unequivocally and exactly intelligible to those whom he addressed. It is especially worthy of notice that in the very two Epistles where, if anywhere, this broader significance of the term is to be traced (Ephesians and Colossians), he lays peculiar emphasis upon the Gentile character of those appealed to. Is it likely that he, a Greek in education and early environment, writing to people Greek in speech and custom, would make use of a well-known Greek word, descriptive of an equally well-known Greek institution, not in the sense familiar to them, but in a technical sense borrowed from the LXX.—a source of which they probably knew nothing?

THE CHURCH OF THE NEW TESTAMENT

Yet it is on so narrow a basis that the conception of a "Hebraic" tinge in the use of the word has been built, and the consequent theory of a Christian church as a riper form of the Jewish, including the world-elect race. The "Hebraic" figment has, as has already been shown, begun to "wax old and vanish away." The conception growing out of it ought also to fade.

Having now asked what the attendant circumstances may lead us to expect as the New Testament meaning of the word *ekklesia*, let us next appeal to the text to learn whether the presumptions raised are justified by the record itself.

III.

NEW TESTAMENT USE OF "ECCLESIA" AND "BASILEIA"

I. COLLATERAL ALLUSION.—We are thus prepared by an impartial inquiry as to the actual meaning of the words under discussion, in the familar speech of the time, to listen to the words of our Lord and his apostles, as nearly as possible in the attitude of those whom they actually addressed. It may fairly be presumed that they will intend us to understand them as the ordinary hearer or reader would naturally have done. If they intend otherwise, this must be clearly shown: it can not be assumed outright.

1. *Greek "assembly."* The allusion to the secular *ekklesia,* in Acts 19: 32, 39, 41, is interesting in two particulars. First, the proposed reference to *"the* regular assembly" (R. V.), "a lawful assembly" (A. V.) —*ennomo*—shows the Ephesian people to be familiar with the ordinary meaning of the term as implying an actual assembly for-

THE CHURCH OF THE NEW TESTAMENT

mally called. An inscription has been found in the very theater where the incident in question occurred, which provides that "a certain silver image of Athene shall be brought and set at every *lawful* [regular] *assembly* [the very words of the New Testament] above the bench where the boys sit" (Peloubet: Acts *in loc.*). It also shows that the word had come to be extended in use, so as to refer to a smaller than the municipal gathering. It was here applied to an unorganized and riotous assembly. That this was an exceptional, although permissible, use of the word is evident from the fact that it is condemned as an "irregular" mob. It is to be remembered that it was to the church in Ephesus that Paul sent his letter in which the word in question is, as we shall see, most disputable in meaning.

The reported use of the word, under the circumstances described, serves to heighten the presumption already reached from the examination of classic and current secular usage outside the New Testament, that the word normally indicates an actual and organized assembly.

2. *The Israelitish "church."* The term *ekklesia* is twice applied to the Israelites;

viz., in Acts 7:38 and in Heb. 2:12. In the one instance it is translated "church," in both versions; in the other it is rendered "church" in the Authorized Version, but "congregation" (with "church" in the margin) in the Revised Version. In the first cited passage Stephen is commenting on the receiving of the law by Moses when with the *"ekklesia* in the wilderness." Turning to the account of this incident in Exodus, we find (Ex. 19:17) that Moses "brought forth the people out of the camp to meet God; and they stood at the nether part of the mount." Here, then, is, again, a distinctly local assembly, formally called out for a specific purpose. There is no allusion to a racial covenant with Abraham, nor to a royal covenant with David, but the *ekklesia* so assembled make for themselves a voluntary and formal covenant with God (Ex. 24:3-8). The term is, therefore, exactly coincident with the Greek in force, and should not be differently rendered.

In the other instance (Heb. 2:12) the expression "in the midst of the *ekklesia* will I praise thee" is borrowed from Ps. 22:22. Here the R. V., while substituting "congregation" for the "church" of the A. V. in

THE CHURCH OF THE NEW TESTAMENT

the citation, rather arbitrarily substitutes "assembly" for the "congregation" of the A. V. Whatever minor variations fancy may suggest for the Englishing of the word in either case, the idea remains the same and inevitable. The singing of praise "in the midst" of the Abrahamic race, of the elect of all ages, or of an invisible or a visible Church universal, is grotesquely inconceivable. In so far as these Old Testament allusions bear at all upon our inquiry, they again confirm expectation that the ordinary popular conception of the Greek word in question will *prima facie* prevail.

3. *The heavenly "Church."* In Heb. 12: 23 the writer refers to the "general assembly [*paneguros*] and church [*ekklesia*] of the firstborn, which are written [who are enrolled—R. V.] in heaven." The accompanying mention of the "heavenly Jerusalem," as well as the words cited, shows that the actual Christian Church is not here alluded to. "It is not to the point," says Sayford in Hastings' Bible Dictionary, "as an instance of a distinctively Christian use of *ekklesia*. It is plain from the connection with *panegurei* that *ekklesia* is here used in a quite general meaning—'assembly,' with-

out reference to its technical Christian significance." Dr. Thayer, in his dictionary, concurs. He decides that "the name is transferred to the assembly of faithful Christians already dead and received into heaven." This passage may, therefore, be ignored as irrelevant in our inquiry as to the nature of the earthly church.

Two interesting suggestions may, however, be noticed in connection with the passage. One is that of the Revisers, in their marginal note; intimating that there is possibility of an alternative translation, thus: "to innumerable hosts, the general *assembly of angels,* and the church of the firstborn," etc. Another hint may be gathered (whether or not this alternative rendering be set aside) from the collocation of *paneguros* and *ekklesia.* The Greek *paneguros* was a festive gathering of all the Greek states, as contrasted with the *ekklesia,* which was confined to one. It is rightly translated "general," as *ekklesia* might rightly be translated "local." Either the "firstborn," gathered out of the earth at last into a single assembly, are set over against the hosts of the redeemed from the whole universe; or the local assemblies (*ekklesiæ*) of earth are represented

THE CHURCH OF THE NEW TESTAMENT

as at last merging into and becoming a *paneguros*. In either case the same general implication once more returns, as to the primary individual meaning of *ekklesia*.

II. EXPLICIT SENSE.—In the great bulk of the instances in which the word *ekklesia* appears in the New Testament, there is no reasonable ground to doubt its pointing to an actual local historical body. The meaning of the word becomes debatable, therefore, in only a comparatively small number of passages—how small is itself a matter of debate, as yet, and, as we shall see, of constantly changing opinion. Let us, then, first note and classify the cases about which there is little or no occasion or disposition to differ in opinion. Then, dismissing these from attention, we may pass to the consideration of those about which question has been raised.

1. *Individual assemblies.* Figures differ slightly in estimating the actual number of instances under each head, because of doubt as to textual legitimacy of the word, or because of divergence of opinion as to classification. I reckon the whole number of appearances of the word in the New Testament at 113. Six of these have already been set aside as collateral in bearing. Of

THE CHURCH AND THE KINGDOM

the remaining 107, I classify ninety-two as clearly carrying the literal and ordinary sense. Only fifteen, therefore, remain to be examined as open to doubt. Of the ninety-two literal references, I find fifty-four to refer to

(1) A local body; as follows:

a. In a private house; *e. g.,* that of Prisca and Aquila (Rom. 16:5). (Four instances.)

b. In a particular city; *e. g.,* "the church which was at Jerusalem" (Acts 8:1). (Of this class I find thirty instances.)

NOTE.—It does not follow that all believers in any city are to be always reckoned as forming one church. It is always a church *"in"* and not *"of"* a city, as Hort notes (*"Ecclesia,"* 114:5); or of persons, as "of the Thessalonians." The "church in the house" seems to have existed in cities to which Epistles were sent. These must have been, in some sense at least, independent bodies.

c. A territorial group; *e. g.,* the "churches of Galatia" (Gal. 1:2). (Twenty instances.) There is only a single instance in which there is question as to the possible organization of believers in a district.

THE CHURCH OF THE NEW TESTAMENT

Where the Authorized Version reads (in Acts 9: 31) "the *churches* of Judæa and Galilee and Samaria," the Revised Version substitutes the singular number, "the *church* of Judæa and Galilee and Samaria."

In the Epistle to the Galatians, written some twenty years later, Paul, referring to the same period, speaks of the "churches of Judæa" (Gal. 1: 22). This either suggests the accuracy of the old version, or that, as Dr. Broadus suggests, the members of the church at Jerusalem, the only one as yet organized, who had reckoned themselves still a part of that body, although widely scattered through the provinces named, now organized themselves into independent bodies, and so became the "churches of Judæa." In any case, the conception of a provincial church is so incongruous with the whole tenor of New Testament history that nobody nowadays seriously contends for its reality. Even were provincial organization to be accepted as having been proven, it would be far from proving also the existence of a world-church. The constant use of the plural in all these passages (churches) indicates the partitive and individual character of the idea conveyed.

THE CHURCH AND THE KINGDOM

2. *Generic title.* In the group of cases now to be cited the word is applied, not to particular existing bodies, but to the institution itself, of which they were representative. It is not a specific body, but the church *as such,* that is meant. Under this head we may include the use of the word

(1) In a distributive sense; *e. g.,* "as I teach everywhere in *every* church" (1 Cor. 4: 17). (Two instances.)

(2) In a collective sense; *e. g.,* "in all the churches" (1 Cor. 7: 17); "neither the churches of God" (1 Cor. 11: 16). (Of this, fourteen cases.)

(3) In a descriptive sense; *e. g.,* "let your women keep silence in the churches" (1 Cor. 14: 34). (Of this usage, twenty-two examples.)

3. *Alleged exceptions.* Some of the passages here included as individual in reference are sometimes claimed to demand a wider interpretation. The number of these passages is comparatively small, and to them we may give closer attention. They are (1) Acts 20: 17. Here the Ephesian elders are said to have been called to "feed the *church of God.*" It is suggested that this august title can not properly attach to a single

THE CHURCH OF THE NEW TESTAMENT

organization, but must have a general reference. But the suggestion seems insignificant. The words are addressed to individual officials to whom was committed the care of a particular company, called in the same verse a "flock"; it was plainly this single flock which they were exhorted to "feed," and not the Christian world at large. The same expression recurs in 1 Thess. 2: 14, where a general reference is precluded not only by the plural form it assumes, but by localization—"the churches of God which are in Judæa."

(2) Rom. 16: 23. "Gaius my host, and of the whole church." It is objected that this can not be limited to the Corinthian church, from which Paul was writing. But Paul has just before (v. 1) called Phœbe a "servant of the church"; this does not mean of the Church universal, but of the "church which is at Cenchreæ," as he immediately adds. In like manner he compliments the local hospitality of the individual who is entertaining him, and who in like manner serves all his brethren. So that the objection seems frivolous.

(3) 1 Cor. 10: 32. "Give no occasion of stumbling, either to Jews, or to Greeks,

or to the church of God." The "church of God," it is argued, must here mean the Church universal, since, like "Jews" and "Greeks," it covers a world-group. But the offense given must needs have been to individual Jews or Greeks, since they could not as a race be thus disturbed by individual conduct. Why, then, must it needs mean more than "do not offend any church or any member of a church"? The fact is that the whole exhortation, as study of the context will make clear, is directed to the regulation of personal conduct toward the different classes of the immediate community.

(4) 1 Cor. 12:28. "God hath set some in the church, first apostles, secondly prophets, thirdly teachers," etc. Inasmuch as apostles were not officials of any particular church, it is inferred that allusion must here be made to the Church as a whole—the world-body. This is, to my mind, the most plausible of the objections as yet encountered. But it does not compel the conclusion supposed to be inevitable. For the writer is speaking, not exclusively of church officials, but of gifts bestowed and functions exercised in connection with the church. "Miracles," "gifts of healing," "divers kinds of

THE CHURCH OF THE NEW TESTAMENT

tongues," were not official. The apostles were "in" the church, not "over" it. Moreover, the term "apostle" is formally applied to an official of the local church in 2 Cor. 8: 23 (R. V.—margin). The whole twelfth chapter of 1 Corinthians is so manifestly local in its drift and statements that it would be incongruous to extend any part of it to a world-wide body.

(5) 1 Cor. 15: 9. "Because I persecuted the church of God." Paul's self-accusation in this passage, repeated verbally in Gal. 1: 13, is alleged to imply that the "church" alluded to was the Christian community at large, ranging far beyond Jerusalem. Now, it is a curious fact that there is no proof that Paul's "persecution" ever went beyond the church at Jerusalem. In Acts 8: 3 it is said that he "made havoc of the church" there. Ananias, when called on to visit Paul, replied to the Lord: "I have heard from many of this man, how much evil he did to thy saints at Jerusalem" (Acts 9: 18). When he began to preach, the people said: "Is not this he that in Jerusalem made havoc of them which called on this name?" In Paul's own defense before Agrippa he emphasizes his cruelties to the "saints" in Jeru-

salem, shutting them up in prison and compelling them to blaspheme. It is true that he adds that "being exceedingly mad against them, I persecuted them even to strange cities." But the word he uses (*dioko*) implies that the objects of his vengeance were still the Jerusalem saints whom he was *pursuing*. So that his "persecution of the church of God" appears to have been limited to the constituency of a single church.

(6) 1 Tim. 3: 14, 15. "These things write I unto thee . . . that thou mayest know how thou oughtest to behave thyself in the house of God, which is the church of the living God, the pillar and ground of the truth" (A. V.); "how men ought to behave *themselves,*" etc. (R. V.). It is singular that any reader of this Epistle should interpret this personal counsel to a local pastor, as to the proper behavior of a pastor or his people in relation to the body to which they both belong, as in any way referring to a world-church. For, in the first place, both "house" (household) and "church" are *anarthrous,* as well as the words following; it should read, properly, *a* house of God, which is *a* church of *a* living God, *a* pillar and stay of the truth. This implies, as Hort con-

cludes, that "Paul's idea is that *each living society* of Christians is a pillar and stay (bulwark) of the truth, as an object of belief and a guide of life for mankind" (*"Eccl.,"* 174).

It would have been useless to instruct Timothy as to the duties of a pastor of the Church universal, for he held no such office, or of the Church invisible, for it has no offices at all. So that this may again be dismissed as in no way antagonizing the conception of the *ekklesia* as primarily and properly concrete and individual in character.

There remain now for consideration only the words of our Lord in Matt. 16: 18 and the use of the word in the Epistles of Ephesians and Colossians. It may be remarked, before beginning to study them, that Dr. Hort, an Anglican, upon strictly exegetic grounds, rejects all except these sources as affording trustworthy grounds on which to base a theory of the Church universal. Dr. Candlish, a Presbyterian, rejects even the critical text in Matthew.

III. DISPUTABLE USE.

1. *The Papal stronghold.* The words of our Lord in Matt. 16: 18, 19 are blazoned

THE CHURCH AND THE KINGDOM

above the high altar of St. Peter's in Rome, and looked to as the charter of the Roman Catholic Church. It is claimed that these words distinctly affirm the Church and the Kingdom to be one, and assign to Peter a common supremacy in this dual organism. Since the Church is acknowledged on all hands to be a visible body, it thereupon follows that the Kingdom is also visible and the Papal supremacy also follows logically, as an equally visible center of world-unity. Those who reject the Papacy still generally emphasize this passage as clearly meant to identify the Church and the Kingdom; but they are not all agreed as to visibility of the universal Church so indicated. The Lutherans, as we here see, deny it; the Presbyterians affirm it (although their Confession describes it as also invisible). Meyrick, in Smith's Bible Dictionary, as we have seen, states confidently that the identity of the two is here "formally, as elsewhere virtually, affirmed." It must be admitted that the collocation of the words and the parallelism of idea in the two verses lend plausibility to the notion of intended unification. But if it be accepted and the reference be to the historic Church, the Romanist would seem to

THE CHURCH OF THE NEW TESTAMENT

have the better of the argument. In any case, these words, which have had so large a place in ecclesiological discussion, are well worthy of careful consideration.

2. *Christ's use of "basileia" and "ekklesia."* Endeavoring to put ourselves, as nearly as possible, in the attitude of those to whom the words were spoken, it will be natural for us to expect that the teacher whom the "common people heard gladly" will use familiar words in a familiar sense. The presumption is strong enough, at least, to require positive evidence to rebut it.

It is observable, to begin with, that the phrase "kingdom of God" is sparsely used outside of the Gospels, and "kingdom of heaven" never. On the other hand, the word *ecclesia,* or church, is found in none of the Gospels except Matthew, and is there attributed to our Lord alone, and in but two instances. This entire advancing change of emphasis from *basileia* to *ecclesia,* in the New Testament, whatever it may imply, ought not to be overlooked. Without assuming fully to interpret its significance, it couples itself suggestively with the fact that our Lord's teaching, as well as his life, as presented to us in the Gospels, is at the

THE CHURCH AND THE KINGDOM

same time characteristically world-wide in bearing, and anticipatory and ideal in character. The Acts and the Epistles, on the other hand, are pre-eminently concrete, immediate and practical in theme and purpose. In the one we see, in the main, the pattern of the ideal man and the ideal society, yet to be realized: in the other we have to do with the growing history of an actual organization, and the current problems and experiences of its living members. The one deals especially with the coming Kingdom, that is to say: the other with the present Church.

We have much larger data for the comparative study of his meaning in the case of *basileia,* than in that of *ecclesia.* For the former word recurs incessantly, and in divers relations, while the latter appears but upon two occasions. In one of these instances only (the crucial passage in Matt. 16: 18, 19) are the two words brought into immediate contact.

One of the first difficulties that confront us in attempting to outline the exact idea coupled by our Lord with the word *basileia* is that, being almost uniformly part of the phrase "kingdom of God" or "kingdom of heaven," the descriptive utterances connected with it are always broad, usually parabolic, and frequently elusive, if not paradoxical, when taken in their literal form.

Some features of his teaching on the subject are clear enough in the light of current usage. Thus the word is employed not only exclusively in the singular, but as if this were its only normal form. To the Roman there could be but one *basileia*, as there was but one Cæsar: correspondingly, to think of two "kingdoms of God," would be to imply two Gods. Etymologically, *basileia* conveys an abstract idea—that of kingship or sovereignty. And this meaning is evidently intended in many passages (*e. g.*, in Matt. 6: 13, "thine *is* the kingdom; *i. e.*, the kingdom *de jure*). It may also take on a chronologic force, designating the visible reign of a particular sovereign. Thus the immediately preceding verse, in the passage just referred to, contains the prayer "Thy kingdom come" (Matt. 6: 10). This conception of the "kingdom of heaven" as a unique world-sovereignty *yet to be established* is, perhaps, more constant than any other, especially in the later New Testament.

The notion of territorial extent was, moreover, inseparable from that of empire.

THE CHURCH AND THE KINGDOM

We are not surprised, therefore, to find that out of "his kingdom" established in the "world-field" are to be "gathered all things that offend, and them which do iniquity" (Matt. 13:41).

But while the juridical, the chronological and the territorial allusions are manifest and apprehensible, there are other hints of a deeper and more mystical purport, in the language used. Thus, while the kingdom is "at hand" (Matt. 4:17), his hearers are remonstrated with for expecting it "immediately to appear" (Luke 19:11). It "cometh not with observation" (Luke 17:20), yet there were some then living who should "not taste of death, till they see the kingdom of God" (Luke 9:27). It was to grow, like the mustard seed, to natural completeness (Matt. 13:32), yet the accompanying parables of the tares and the net show that completeness is to be reached only through supernatural invention (Matt. 13:41, 49). None but the regenerate can enter the kingdom (John 3:5), yet some are to be gathered out of it who shall be "cast into a furnace of fire" (Matt. 13:42). These, like the statement that "whosoever will save his life shall lose it," and other apparently con-

THE CHURCH OF THE NEW TESTAMENT

tradictory affirmations of Scripture, are, of course, not contradictory in fact, but only in form. Like a "fault" in mining, which is said to occur usually where the ore is richest, they baffle that they may stimulate us to find the deeper meaning hinted at. It should be remembered that it was in connection with the giving of the "parables of the kingdom" that our Lord intimated a purposed reserve in his teachings. He hid the truth in parables, as he hides the grain in the husk, *from* the listless or self-sufficient, *for* the docile and diligent (Matt. 13: 10-15). It was in like connection that he uttered those hesitating and apparently deprecating words, as if about to undertake the impracticable, "Whereunto shall we liken the kingdom of God, and with what comparison shall we compare it?" (Mark 4: 30).

From this last despondent cry we may get some notion, at the same time, of the profundity of the theme with which he was attempting to grapple, and of the difficulties which met him in trying to make it intelligible to his auditors; partly because of the inherent infirmity of human speech, partly because of the prepossessions of the people before him. The Jewish conception of the

THE CHURCH AND THE KINGDOM

"kingdom of heaven" was coupled inseparably with a restoration of the splendor of the Solomonic reign, rising upon the ruins of the prostrate fabric of imperial Rome. The human idea of *basileia* was, at the best, everywhere defiled by earthly and carnal associations. It suggested a visible ruler, the obtrusive pageantry of throne and court, and external apparatus of legislative and administrative control, and the like. But muddy and inadequate as the simile was, it was the fittest available, and seemingly providentially so. For there was in the popular mind a dim conception of an intangible, indescribable somewhat, which was behind and greater than the temporary occupant of the imperial throne. "Divus" Cæsar was worshiped, not in his personal capacity, but as the *simulacrum* of that immortal, inflexible, all-pervasive, irresistible, but invisible, reality known vaguely as the "empire," the "state," the "law." Thousands who had never actually seen Cæsar or Rome, had been laid hold of in imagination by the familiar motto, *"Ubi Cæsar, ibi Roma,"* and had realized the intangible presence of both. What could have been seized upon as furnishing a better incipient, although feeble,

THE CHURCH OF THE NEW TESTAMENT

analogue of that "kingdom which ruleth over all," the august reality of which transcends the capacity of definition or metaphor, and must appeal to the human imagination in inevitable paradox?

We are thus forced to rest in the conclusion that the "kingdom" in question, whose domain is "within," which is "not of this world," which "cometh not with observation," which is never spoken of as to be "built" (as the "church" is), neither is, nor was it intended by human agency ever to be made, an external or discernible earthly entity. It sets before us an ideal, forever transcending our power fully to grasp, forever stimulating us to aspiration, prayer and expectation, but the realization of which the Lord alone must "hasten in his time." Only when the New Jerusalem shall "descend from God out of heaven," can the new kingdom take on, visibly, concrete form, and become capable of confident definition. Our Lord's allusions are a preliminary "apocalypse," and the apocalypse needs itself yet to be revealed.

Turning now to our Lord's references to the *ecclesia*, we find no difference of opinion as to his intent in one of the instances where the word occurs (Matt. 18: 17). There is some conflict of judgment as to the particular local body indicated, whether the existing synagogue or the coming individual church, but none whatever as to the reference of the word, in accordance with common usage, to *some* local assembly. It is to be remarked that the definite article is here used—*"the"* church—so that the uniform interpretation of the passage in the manner above stated is a sufficient answer to those who deny that the generic or partitive sense can ever attach to *ecclesia* under such circumstances. If the reference be to the synagogue, it is of considerable importance, as showing that the words *sunagoge* and *ecclesia* were now synonymous. That this was so, we may infer from the use of the two words as equivalent by James in his Epistle, before noted. But the circumstance is especially useful here, as preparing us to understand the force of the word in the other passage in Matthew yet to be considered. For *sunagoge* was used in the Septuagint as the synonym of *ecclesia*. Now, if the one word, which had formerly meant the national assembly, had unequivocally sunk to the limits

THE CHURCH OF THE NEW TESTAMENT

of the village body, by what kind of logic can it be contended that the other word, still remaining a synonym, had retained its national reference only? It seems more natural to accept the suggestion that the synagogue is, in fact, here meant, inasmuch as the phrase "the *ecclesia*" suggests an existing and readily identifiable institution; whereas in the other passage the coming Christian Church is designated, as if in contrast, as "MY *ecclesia*."

But it is not very material what particular individual body may have been intended. The expectation with which our examination began is, in this place, at least justified. The meaning of the word uniformly prevalent throughout the Greek-speaking world is employed, as if of course. It need not surprise us that this should be thought proper in addressing a Jewish company. It is doubtful whether modern scholars have adequately recognized the extent to which the Hellenization of the eastern half of the empire, including its Jewish constituency, had gone. The existence of the Septuagint and its frequent adoption, instead of the Hebrew, in Palestinian synagogues, the rise of the synagogue and of the

THE CHURCH AND THE KINGDOM

Rabbinic school and dialectic, to say nothing of abundant contemporary historic evidence, show the almost universal familiarity of the people with Greek ideas. At all events, any who could have been influenced in interpretation by the example of the Septuagint writers, must have been sufficiently familiar with Greek to read it. The Seventy had, it is true, when seeking for a fit Greek word to translate the Hebrew name of the national assembly, accepted *ecclesia* as the nearest analogue, alternating it with *sunagoge,* substituted when used in the larger sense. There was no incongruity in this: for the "congregation" held the same relation to the Jewish state that the *ecclesia* did to the Greek. The fact that there had once been only one Jewish *ecclesia,* while among the Greeks the number of such bodies was limited only by the number of states, should not blind us to the determining circumstance that in neither case was the body in question thought of as a universal, or world-wide, assembly. Its meaning was in either case local and partitive. But the national Jewish assembly had long been lost from sight. Instead of the one *ecclesia* or *sunagoge,* there had arisen as many individual synagogues

THE CHURCH OF THE NEW TESTAMENT

as there were city neighborhoods or village communities. The alternate name must have shrunk to the dimensions of the fact. We know this to have been true of the synagogue: we can not safely doubt it as to the *ecclesia*. The Greek *ecclesia* had likewise suffered specialization, as we have already seen, having been in later times applied familiarly to local associations. It is not without significance that, in choosing between the two words, our Lord should prefer the more thoroughly Gentile word *ecclesia* to the *sunagoge,* which latter was more purely Jewish in association: for the one was the direct political antipode, as the other was not, of *basileia*.

3. *The critical passage.* We come, then, to the study of the famous passage (Matt. 16: 18, 19) about the correct interpretation of which in detail there has been a world of controversy, and on which so much depends. If the authority of current Greek usage and the concurrent testimony of the Gospels themselves, in so far as they supply any definite precedent for our guidance, are to count for anything, we shall expect to find that *basileia* here, as uniformly elsewhere, carries with it the notion of a world-power,

single, exclusive, monocratic: while *ecclesia* will presumably retain its contrasted distributive idea, that of a local assembly, one of many, and democratic. A sudden absolute reversal of the meaning of either of the words, for which no single precedent can be cited, is admissible only under the pressure of cogent evidence from the passage itself. Is such evidence forthcoming?

Nobody questions that *basileia* is used in its familiar sense; the qualifying words "of heaven" contrasting the world-dominion of God with that of Cæsar. Nor is there room for doubt as to the personal destination of the "keys," which are explicitly said to be given to Peter. But when we come to *ecclesia,* we are asked to assume that it has arbitrarily reversed its accustomed meaning, thus becoming identifiable, if not identical, with *basileia,* of which it had hitherto been always the antithesis. With this unexplained departure from settled usage at once arise questions of chronic dispute. Is the world-church identical with the world-kingdom? Is it visible or invisible? Is the "rock" on which it is built Peter, or his confession, or Christ?

Let us examine the language under the

theory that the uniform meaning of the words remains undisturbed, and see if we encounter insuperable objections. Notice, first, that Christ applies to the *ecclesia* the qualification "my," as if contrasting it with some other recognizable body: that he speaks of it as to be "built": and that he declares "the gates of Hades shall not prevail against it" (R. V.). Neither of these particulars is expressly affirmed of the "kingdom of heaven." The most natural subject of comparison suggested by the word "my" would be the only existing religious *ecclesia* known to those he addressed, the synagogue.

He was then referring to the *ecclesia* he was about to found as an institution characteristically different from the familiar Jewish one. There is nothing unusual, in the New Testament or outside of it, in such a generic or representative use of terms. When James, addressing all the Jewish Christians of the Dispersion, refers to "your synagogue" (Jas 2:2), and a little later to "the elders of the church" (5:14), does anybody imagine him to conceive of a *universal* synagogue or *universal* church, rather than any church or synagogue as a characteristic institution? Archbishop Whately

THE CHURCH AND THE KINGDOM

reminds us, when discussing this very question, that Thucydides often alludes to *"the* democracy" or *"the* oligarchy," when referring to individual bodies in the various Greek cities "formed on similar principles," without the suspicion that he could be understood to imply a pan-hellenic democracy or oligarchy. "So doubtless ought we to interpret the Scripture writers," he adds, when they refer in like manner to "the church."

If we understand the "rock," here mentioned, as the confession just uttered by Peter, the point of contrast between the coming church and the existing synagogue becomes more apparent. For just this definite confession of faith in Christ as Messiah, visibly reiterated in baptism, is the essential foundation of a normal Christian church; the birthright constitution of the synagogue being repudiated. We have authority enough for that interpretation, if we may accept the testimony of Archbishop Kenrick, of the Roman Catholic Church. For in his address prepared for (but not delivered at) the Vatican Council, he tells us that forty-four Fathers and Doctors approve it, against seventeen who refer the term to Peter, and sixteen who refer it to Christ himself: a

THE CHURCH OF THE NEW TESTAMENT

decided majority being in favor of the former. The introduction of the word "rock" is, no doubt, due to a play of words suggested by Peter's peculiar name; but no satisfactory reason has ever been given for the arbitrary change of gender from *Petron* to *Petran*. If we suppose the reference to be to *omologian,* which is feminine, the change would have some pretext at least.

The allusion to "building" suggests another point of distinction between the "church" and the "kingdom." The latter is never referred to in Scripture as "built" or as taking organic immediate form in any decisive way. But the local church is characteristically and incessantly described as the subject of "edification" (the same Greek word). The Ephesian church is addressed as "built upon the foundation of the apostles and prophets [that is, evidently, the foundation *laid by* them. Cf. Tit. 3:5], Christ Jesus himself being the chief corner-stone." To understand the church here referred to as the local body brings the figurative allusion precisely in line with its use throughout the New Testament.

The declaration that the "gates of Hades shall not prevail against it" need occasion

THE CHURCH AND THE KINGDOM

no difficulty, if we understand it as promising that the Christian Church as an actual institution shall never be finally extirpated. The language does not compel the inference of uninterrupted visible continuity. It implies a matching of forces in which the Church shall victoriously survive. In the next verses (Matt. 16:21) our Lord announces his own approaching subjection to the power of death, but adds that he shall "be raised again the third day." The "gates of Hades" could not "prevail" against him; death could not permanently shut him in, for he could not be "holden of it." His prophecy, therefore, would be fairly fulfilled if the individual church as such do not perish absolutely, and everywhere.

Finally, the universalization of the Church and its identification with the kingdom of heaven, with the prolonged Jewish *regime*, or with the elect of all ages, loads the passage with chronological and metaphorical incongruities of formidable character. If "kingdom" and "church" are identical, both must be built on Peter, to satisfy the Romish theory, and the "keys" of the structure thus appear to be given to its own corner-stone. If the new kingdom

THE CHURCH OF THE NEW TESTAMENT

and the Israelitish are identical, then Peter becomes the foundation stone of an organization already centuries old. If the whole body of the elect be built on Peter or on his confession of the incarnate Messiah, then he must be file-leader of an immeasurable procession starting beyond the flood.

No such difficulties attend the construction of the language here proposed. It simply supposes our Lord consistent with himself, and with the ordinary usages of speech, assuming that he whom "the common people heard gladly" would not wantonly use words in a strange sense which would inevitably perplex or mislead the common man.

4. *Apostolic usage.* Passing on from the Gospels to *the remaining books of the New Testament,* in our inquiry as to the meaning of *ecclesia,* we shall find the field of research materially limited by the concessions of the latest critical scholarship. If it seem presumptuous to question the validity of the long confidently cherished notion that the word does sometimes, at least, refer to a Church universal, a notion still held by the bulk of interpreters, it must be remembered that one of the chief incentives to doubt has been

furnished by a change in the set of the tide of opinion among interpreters themselves. We have seen that the equally long established and unquestioned notion of the identity of "church" and "kingdom" has been of late bluntly challenged as an unverified assumption, and, for lack of ability to justify itself, has been repudiated by a steadily increasing list of reputable authorities. But the notions of universality and identity are twin-born, and have always been inseparably associated in thought. It seems inevitable that the rejection of the one as spurious should entail suspicion of the other. Such suspicion is abundantly justified by the incipient tendency above referred to, manifest in the

5. *Adverse results of recent textual study.* As a fair exponent of the ripest results of critical investigation of the text, we may safely accept Dr. F. J. A. Hort, who has summed up the results of inquiry in his book on "The Christian *Ecclesia*." Dr. Hort has become famous in connection with the production of the most authoritative revision of the Greek text of the New Testament, and stands in the front rank of Greek scholars. As an official in a

THE CHURCH OF THE NEW TESTAMENT

national church, he can not be suspected of bias against the national or universal theory. It will be only fair to assume that he will not assent to any interpretation that may even indirectly cast discredit upon that theory, unless compelled by rigorous exegetical necessity. Turning to his pages, we discover:

First. A sweeping rejection of all proof-texts hitherto cited from the Acts and Epistles, except those found in Ephesians and Colossians. In these he finds "for the first time in the Acts and Epistles the *ecclesia* spoken of in the sense of the one universal *ecclesia*": and "this is confined to the twin Epistles to Ephesians and Colossians." In this judgment Dr. Hort is confirmed by the new Hastings' Bible Dictionary (issued under the associate supervision of scholars such as Davidson, Driver and Swete). The article upon this topic contains the following statement: "Not until late in the Epistles is the *ecclesia* called outright the 'body of Christ' (Eph. 1: 23; 4: 12; 5: 23; Col. 1: 18, 24; 2: 19). In the earlier Epistles it is the vague 'we,' 'you;' *i. e.*, primarily the community to which the apostle is writing, although the secondary idea of the whole church was probably present to his mind (Rom. 12: 5; 1 Cor. 12: 15, 27. Cf. 6: 15)."

It is unnecessary to go over the whole list of passages formerly adduced as carrying the universal sense, but now dismissed on critical grounds as inappropriate. A few instances will serve to indicate the nature of the reasons assigned for their abandonment. In the work last named, for instance, the notable passage in Heb. 12: 23, before noted, is ruled out as "not to the point as an instance of a distinctively Christian use of *ecclesia*. It is plain from the connection with *panegurei* that *ecclesia* is used here in a quite general meaning, assembly, without reference to its technical Christian significance." Dr. Hort finds eleven varying phases of meaning, all of which point to the local body, except one ("the one universal *ecclesia*"), confined to the two Epistles above specified. Paul's allusion to the "church of God" (Gal. 1: 13) applies to "the original *ecclesia* of Jerusalem or Judea, at a time when there was no other." In Rom. 16: 23 "the church" is "any church." In Acts 20: 28 the "church of God" is "the one universal *ecclesia* as represented in the local, individual *ecclesia*." There are but three

THE CHURCH OF THE NEW TESTAMENT

cases (1 Cor. 10: 32; 11: 22, and probably 12: 28) to which this last metaphorical implication is attached, and it will be noticed that the *direct* reference is even here to the local body.

Second. The changes in interpretation, due to recent textual and grammatic recension, are almost without exception favorable to the distributive as against the universal sense of the word. Observe the bearing of the following changes introduced by the Revisers. In Eph. 2: 21 *"all the* building" has now become *"each several* building." In Eph. 3: 15 *"the whole* family" now reads *"every* family." In 1 Cor. 3: 16 and 2 Cor. 6: 16 *"a temple"* has been substituted for *"the temple."* In some instances they have inconsistently retained the definite article where, according to Dr. Hort, the form of the Greek makes it inadmissible. For example, *"the* church of God" in 1 Tim. 3: 5, as well as in verse 15, should be *"a* church of God." He thinks it more accurate, also, to render Col. 3: 15 "called in *a* body" than, as now, "in *one* body."

The significance of some of these changes, as affecting the question under consideration, will be at once apparent. A careful study of the context will show others not less important.

As bearing upon the general antithesis of *basileia* and *ecclesia,* here contended for, it may be worthy of notice that while the tendency of textual emendation has been to confine *ecclesia* more rigorously to its original local and partitive sense, the two changes in the case of *basileia* have looked in the direction of singleness and universality. In Rev. 1:6 the Revisers have given *"a kingdom"* instead of *"kings,"* while in the same book (11:15) the plural *"kingdoms"* has given way to the singular *"kingdom."*

Third. With this relinquishment of successive outworks has come a practical abandonment of what has hitherto been treated as the central position: it is no longer claimed that the universal is the primary or ordinary meaning of *ecclesia.* Whether tested by an etymological or historic standard, it limits itself inexorably to the partitive sense. Primarily it was an actual assembly of an individual group: it was, in time, extended also, subordinately, to a company accustomed to assemble: but it never referred to a world-body nor to an ideal assembly.

THE CHURCH OF THE NEW TESTAMENT

There are two words in Hebrew, according to Dr. Hort, referring to the "congregation" of Israel, which are of especial interest in this connection. The first (*edhah*) designates "the society itself, formed by the children of Israel or their representative heads, *whether assembled or not assembled."* The second (*qahal*) is *"properly their actual meeting together."* The two words sometimes occur together and are equivalent to "the *assembly* of the congregation "(italics not in original). Now it is the word *qahal* for which *ecclesia* was chosen by the Seventy as an equivalent; and for obvious reasons. The Hebrew and the Greek word each came from a root which signified to call or summon. In the case of the Greek "the original *calling out* is simply the calling of the citizens of a Greek town out of their houses by the herald's trumpet to summon them to the assembly: and Numbers 10 shows that the summons to the Jewish assembly was made in the same way."

Both the Hebrew words referred to are "mainly confined to the historical parts of the historical book. They have no place in the greater prophecies having what we call a Messianic import. From all parts of the

THE CHURCH AND THE KINGDOM

Book of Isaiah they are both entirely absent." Their use, therefore, "is almost wholly historical, not ideal or doctrinal." Schurer cites certain passages from the Talmud to show that *qahal* came to "have a high ideal character": but these, as Dr. Hort assures us, "do not at all bear him out."

In the later historical books, he finds indications that *qahal* (and its equivalent *ecclesia*) had come to include the idea represented by the other words mentioned, and *ecclesia* and *sunagoge* had thus become closely allied in sense. In the Apocrypha *sunagoge* already appears to be shrinking into a name of the local congregation. That the word *ecclesia* had shrunk correspondingly in Jewish conception is implied in the statement that "the actual precept (in Matt. 18: 17) is hardly intelligible if what the *ecclesia* meant is not the Jewish community, apparently the Jewish local community, to which the injured person and the offender both belonged."

We may thus appeal to the authority of this eminent critic in confirmation of the suggestion herein already offered, that, to the mind of a Greek-speaking Jew in our Lord's time, the word *ecclesia* would natu-

THE CHURCH OF THE NEW TESTAMENT

rally suggest the synagogue, and therefore couple itself primarily with the notion of a local organization.

Under this changed aspect of the case, it is manifest that the burden of proof shifts to the shoulders of him who will impose upon a familiar word an unusual, and, in the first instance, improbable, sense.

Fourth. In accordance with what has just been said, Dr. Hort admits the necessity of finding some other than etymological, grammatical or historical grounds on which to rest his continued faith in Paul's intent to refer to a Church universal. This is *not* the *"proper original force"* of *ecclesia:* it is not traceable to "current usage": it has been always limited by Paul himself to a local organization which has "a corresponding unity of its own: each is a body of Christ and a sanctuary of God." But, upon reaching Ephesians, he discovers the idea of "the one universal *ecclesia*" for the first time, "and it comes more from the *theological* than from the *historical* side; *i. e.,* less from the circumstances of the actual Christian community than from a development of thought respecting the place and office of the Son of God. His Headship was felt to involve the unity of all those who were united in Him." This language is somewhat confusing. Does he mean that Paul is still speaking of the local body as a *symbol* or *type* of the heavenly church? If the church referred to be not *historical,* it can hardly be *actual* at all; yet he seems to imply in what follows that the language directly refers to a present reality; for he speaks of it just after as an earthly "community." Here is again proposed a novel and highly precarious form of exegetical procedure. Instead of resorting to etymology, historic precedent, the usage of contemporaries or of the writer himself, or to adjacent circumstance, to settle the meaning of a word, resort is had to an inverted process, and an unprecedented meaning is thus reflected upon it by theological inference. It is not remarkable that the learned exegete should, by his roundabout process, reach at the end of his discussion only the halting conclusion that "it may be regarded as morally certain that the *Ecclesia* here intended is not a local community, but the community of Christians as a whole." Moral certainty falls a good way short of demonstrative certainty. The qualifying word implies hesitation and in-

THE CHURCH OF THE NEW TESTAMENT

vites suspense of judgment. There is no such qualifying word used, or thought of, when the question of the local sense of the word has been under notice.

It comes to this, then, that the notion of a universal Church, as derived from the New Testament, has thus far rested largely on mistaken citation of inapplicable texts, that advancing study of the text has robbed it of some supports which in the older translation seemed to buttress it, and that its latest advocate feels compelled to rest his defense of it solely on the probable force of theoretic inference.

It can not be unreasonable to see in this backward trend an occasion for distrust, and for suspecting that the process of revision of judgment ought to go still further.

The admission that the primary sense of *ecclesia* is local, coupled with the recognition of an increasingly preponderant number of instances of its use in that sense in the New Testament, tend strongly toward the repudiation of the universal meaning still attached to it in a few remaining passages. For the extraordinary is *prima facie* the improbable, and requires extraordinary evidence. The natural presumption is in favor of any interpretation which does not require the sudden and incongruous introduction of an unfamiliar meaning. Bearing this in mind, let us ask if there be not

6. *Difficulties in this interpretation of "ecclesia" in Ephesians and Colossians.* Dr. Hort does not conceal from himself the difficulties that attend the effort to fix upon Paul's use of the word in these Epistles a meaning discordant with his own hitherto absolutely uniform, as well as with "current," usage. This is arbitrary and indefensible, unless compelled by extraneous considerations.

These considerations he finds in three circumstances. 1. That in the course of his teaching Paul has come to dwell upon "the relation of the Son of God to the constitution of the universe, and to the course of human history, and in connection with such themes it was but natural that the *Ecclesia* of God should find place." 2. That "to St. Paul, when writing this Epistle (Ephesians) 'the *Ecclesia*' was a kind of symbol or visible expression of that wondrous 'mystery,' to use his own word, which had been hidden throughout the ages, but was not made manifest; that the Gentiles were fellow-heirs and of the same body": for "He is our peace and hath made them both one." 3. That he was writing from Rome and by the "impressiveness of the Empire" he "must have been vividly reminded of the already existing unity which comprehended both Jew and Gentile under bond of subjection to the emperor at Rome, and similarity and contrast would alike suggest that a truer unity bound together in one society all believers in the crucified Lord." Thus "in Ephesians and Colossians the change [*i. e.,* in meaning] comes not so much by an expansion or extension of the thought of each local *ecclesia* as a body over a wider sphere as by way of corollary or application, so to speak, of larger and deeper thoughts on the place of Christ in the universal economy of things, antecedent not only to the Incarnation, but to the whole course of the world."

The circumstances named, and especially the admission that the new conception of *ecclesia* is not an "expansion or extension" of the old, suggest the illegitimacy of the proposed interpretation, when considered from two distinct points of view.

First. It would be a palpable violation of the laws of speech, quite unfairly attrib-

THE CHURCH AND THE KINGDOM

uted to Paul, to suppose that he has substituted an entirely different meaning, rather than one normally developed, metaphorically or otherwise, from the old.

Second. It would impose upon the word not simply an alien meaning, but one diametrically opposite to its natural sense. The precise point of contrast between *basileia* and *ecclesia* is, that the former does, as the latter does not, derive unity from a central personality. But the world-fellowship just alluded to, which involves a "mystery," which springs out of the headship of Christ, and which is suggested by the rival imperial unity of Rome, manifestly brings before us that very *basileia* of which Christ so often spoke. The identity of the *basileia* with the *ecclesia,* Dr. Hort has already emphatically declared to be unjustifiable. Paul, in Colossians, speaks of the great company of the redeemed as translated into the "kingdom" (1: 13), and afterwards, in the same chapter (and apparently as discriminating the two), speaks of the "church" (1: 18). For *ecclesia* incontinently to take on the sense of *basileia* would be as unnatural as for "democracy" to ask to be understood as equivalent to "monarchy."

THE CHURCH OF THE NEW TESTAMENT

Third. But this is not the only incongruity entailed by the proposed rendering. The attempt to define the constituency of the universal *ecclesia* brings new trouble. "There is no indication that St. Paul regarded the conditions of membership in the universal *Ecclesia* as differing from the conditions of membership in the local *ecclesiæ*." On this basis it becomes impossible to suppose it made up of local bodies as such, or that it is invisible, or limited to the elect, or wholly in the heavens. All this is distinctly affirmed, and buttressed by confirmatory words from Paul. "The members which make up the one *Ecclesia* are not communities, but individual men. The one *Ecclesia* includes all members of all partial *ecclesiæ*; but its relations to them all are direct, not mediate." The learned author here recedes apparently from his affirmation that the larger is not a mere expansion of the smaller body: for in determining the features and gauging the membership of the former, he makes the latter an inexorable pattern. The universal *ecclesia* must be earthly, visible, and made up of individuals, since the local *ecclesia* is so. But in carrying out the parallel there is an unfortunate hiatus. For he has again and again declared it to be essential to the very being of an *ecclesia* that it should be an organized body. The Jewish *ecclesia* was "no mere agglomeration of men." Speaking of the church at Ephesus, he remarks that "it would seem as though he (Paul) dreaded the very semblance of representing an *Ecclesia* of God as intended to be a shapeless crowd of like and equal units." When the seven deacons were chosen, it was a "sign that the *Ecclesia* was to be an *Ecclesia* indeed, not a mere horde of men ruled absolutely by the Apostles, but a true body politic." But in what sense can "all the members of all the churches" be said to form a "body politic"? Scattered and unrelated individuals, however personally visible, do not constitute a visible *ecclesia*. The Church of Rome alone can pretend to be the universal *ecclesia* here contended for, and that comes short of the standard, in that it does not take in "all the members of all the churches." There is no actual *ecclesia* such as the definition, consistently completed, demands.

Fourth. But, again, it is found impossible to interpret all the figures employed by Paul in these Epistles in the universal sense.

THE CHURCH OF THE NEW TESTAMENT

The representation of the *ecclesia* as the "body" and the "wife" of Christ are supposed to refer to the Church universal, but "if we are not to disregard both grammar and natural sense," we must interpret the "temple" of the local body. "The thought of a universal spiritual temple is, to say the least, not definitely expressed anywhere by Paul." In this particular Dr. Hort abandons the position of Meyer and other earlier exegetes, who held that Paul, as a Jew, could not have tolerated the notion of more than one temple. The new reading *"each several* building" seems to compel reference to the single church, which "groweth into an holy temple" of itself, rather than to a conglomeration of many buildings growing into one—an incoherent figure. The same principle applies in the case of the "household" (Eph. 2:19), which seems to be equally limited to the partitive sense by the expression in 3:15, *"every* family in heaven and on earth." The local body is specifically referred to in Col. 4:15, 16, where he speaks of the *ecclesia* in the "house" of Nymphas and that "of the Laodiceans." In the body of both Epistles, it can not be denied that his remarks are generally localized by the constant use of "we," "you" and the like, as well as by the discussion of relations and exhortation to duties peculiar to personal fellowship in a single body. So that the universal sense of the word is not constant, even in this narrow range. The apostle "glides" from local to universal, to borrow Dr. Hort's own term, and recedes again to the local. That this hypothesis attributes to Paul a most unnatural vacillation in the use of terms, and that it gives too much play to the caprice of a slippery fancy in translation, is plain. For if there is any part of the Epistle to the Ephesians in which the stress of theological argument should compel the introduction of the new sense of universality, it must be in the second and third chapters, where the "mystery" of the fellowship of Jew and Gentile, through the unifying grace of Christ, is most emphasized. But it is precisely here that the intractable figure of "household" and "temple" occur: and, notably enough, they are used of the local church as if co-ordinately with "the body" (3:6), which is claimed to have been used in 1:23, in a sense unquestionably universal.

Fifth. But there is still another difficulty

THE CHURCH OF THE NEW TESTAMENT

in the interpretation by theological indirection instead of exegetical principle. The argument for universality on this basis proves too much. It is urged that the immense range of the Apostle's thought in Eph. 1: 10, 22, 23 and Col. 1: 18-20, coupled as it is with "the body, the church," compels the enlargement of our view of the latter commensurately with "the place of Christ in the universal economy of things." In that case *ecclesia* can no longer be limited to earth or to the membership of visible churches, but as "the fulness of him that filleth all in all," but must become identical with the universe: since, in the universe, Christ "is before all things, and in him *all things consist.*"

Before accepting as "morally certain" an interpretation of Paul's language which would make him, in these Epistles, suddenly defy "current usage" to which he had hitherto rigidly conformed, ignore every precedent which he had himself established, and introduce a new and arbitrary sense into the word (for it is "not an expansion or extension" of its familiar sense that is proposed)—this new sense to be subtly alternated with the old, throughout the discussion

—we may reasonably pause to ask whether the structure and phraseology of the text compel this extraordinary interpretation.

7. *A more rational view.* In the first place, then, is there anything in the scope of the Apostle's thought, or in the form of its expression, absolutely inconsistent with the retention of the familiar local sense of *ecclesia;* by such retention harmonizing its meaning throughout the New Testament? It is plausibly urged that the reference to "the church" as "his body, the fulness of him that filleth all in all," and the declaration that Christ is "head over all things to the church," taken in connection with the broad sweep of the terms in which Christ is alluded to as having reconciled "all things unto himself" (including the making of the Jew and Gentile "twain, one new man"), forbid the notion that he can be referring to the insignificant local church. But the conclusion indicated is not irresistible. It does not follow that because a truth or fact is universal in character, it must express itself through a vehicle universal in extent. The law of the heavenly worlds is revealed in the raindrop. The Son of God was "revealed" in Paul. God is "glorified" in his individual

saints. If it be thought strange that a local body should be described as manifesting the "fulness" of God, let it be noticed that in Col. 2: 9, 10 the *"fulness of God"* is said to have dwelt *"bodily"* in Christ, it being added that "in him *ye* are made *full*": and that in Eph. 3: 19 the prayer is offered that *"ye* may be filled unto all the *fulness of God."* It has been sometimes insisted that the resort to such figures as "body," "temple" and "wife" cuts off the possibility of local, which must be multiple, reference; since there was but one temple, and consistency of metaphor required but a single body or wife. Dr. Hort does not delude himself with this sophistical argument, for he recognizes the conclusiveness of the answer, that the Apostle has elsewhere uniformly spoken of the individual church as *"a* body of Christ," *"a* temple," *"a* virgin": and that in Ephesians *"a* holy temple" (2: 21) refers to the Ephesian church, while the Colossians are, in like manner, said to have been "called in *a* body" (3: 15)—at least, he so translates the latter clause. As to the breaking down of the wall of partition between Jew and Gentile, and between alien classes of all sorts, it would seem that the

THE CHURCH AND THE KINGDOM

local church was the chief, if not the only, agency through which that great change was intended to become manifest. It does not appear that racial, social or civic distinctions at large were directly interfered with by Christianity, except as these hindered equality in the single "household of faith." Paul urged Titus to require "subjection to rulers" in civic affairs, sent back Onesimus to Philemon, consented to the circumcision of the Jewish-born Timothy, although he resented the suggestion in the case of the Gentile Titus, and himself shaved his head and took a vow, which he would have denounced in a Gentile. He rebuked Peter, not because he would not eat with Greeks in general, but because he refused to fraternize with Gentile members of the Antiochean church. All that is said in Ephesians of the Gentiles as "fellow-citizens with the saints, and of the household of God," "fellow-heirs, and fellow-members of the body," as "members one of another," and reconciled "both in one body unto God," finds illustration and confirmation in the local church at Ephesus, as it could not find in the leveling or obliteration of established distinctions of birth or rank in the outside world, even

THE CHURCH OF THE NEW TESTAMENT

among "members of Christian churches."

In the second place, does the inherent force of the symbols chosen encourage the notion of universality, invisible or otherwise? The coincident symbolic use of "body" and "temple" has already occurred, in our Lord's allusion to his own incarnate form (John 2: 19-21). But the very essence of incarnation, as a "manifestation of God in the flesh," involved local and visible tangibility. (Cf. 2 Pet. 1: 16; 1 John 1: 1.) Closely allied to the idea of the temple is that of "building," which is applied to the coming "church" (Matt. 16: 18). All these allusions point irresistibly to a concrete organism. In that sense they are taken up in the Epistles and applied in detail to the local church. "Edification" (or building) is the constantly recurring term descriptive of the processes by which the individual members of the single community are to adjust themselves to each other for the development of the symmetrical unity of the body to which they belong. Of the more than twenty instances in which this word occurs, only four are found in the Ephesians. All except two of these instances are admitted without question to apply to the local body. The local organization is confessedly spoken of (Eph. 2: 21) as a "several *building.*" But afterward we read of the *"jointing together* [*katartismon*] of the saints, unto the work of ministering, unto the *building up* of the body of Christ": and of "the body *fitly framed* and *knit together.*" And this is alleged to refer to the universal "body." But, aside from the fact that this figurative language is coupled directly with "we" and "ye," the phraseology implies a continuity of the subject of thought, the "body" having taken the place of the "temple" of chapter 2; and referring, therefore, still to the Ephesian church. The fact that it is here *"the* body," instead of *"a* body," is not significant, in view of what has already been said as to the use of the definite article, which often points to the specific body as representative of a class.

In the third place, regard ought to be had, in translation, to the essential, as discriminated from the incidental, features of the thing referred to. We must not forget the sage remark of Aristotle that undue expansion of the limits of a thing, whereby it becomes incapable of performing its characteristic functions, may destroy the identity

THE CHURCH OF THE NEW TESTAMENT

of the thing itself. Every definition must be rejected, therefore, that lies open to this criticism. A perverted gospel, Paul said, is "no gospel." The functions of an *ecclesia*, as clearly and uniformly set forth in the New Testament, are pre-eminently two: "edification" of its individual constituents, and "manifestation" of the educating and unifying power of the gospel to those without. But neither of these is possible, except in case of a company among whom intimacy of relation and organized activity makes mutual influence possible; and whose "unity of the spirit in the bond of peace" can become the subject of external recognition.

A Church universal, composed of a disintegrated, unorganized throng of "members of all the churches," is from the functional point of view inconceivable. And how could an indistinguishable, unrecognizable company of God's elect, the invisible Church, serve either the one purpose of a church or the other. A perverted *ecclesia* is, to borrow Paul's phraseology, no *ecclesia*.

Finally, some attention must be paid, in determining the force of terms, to the peculiar genius of Christianity, as compared

THE CHURCH AND THE KINGDOM

with Judaism. Judaism was aggregative and centripetal in organization: Christianity is individualizing and centrifugal. The Old Testament is mainly a national history: the New Testament begins with a fourfold personal biography, and passes on to personal Epistles addressed to local communities. Men were tethered into corporate unity, in the old order, by involuntary entanglement in the mesh of consanguinity, and promise and privilege were tribal covenants "running with the blood," rather than individual gifts. Under the new, every man must believe and obey for himself, and "work out his own salvation" as a "member of a body of Christ." If the Jews had but one temple, it must be remembered that Christ foretold its destruction and the rightful worship of God everywhere; and that Christianity did not come to its best until it was destroyed. Christianity did not take its departure from the one temple, but from the many synagogues. It was not simply an outgrowth from, but rather a reaction against, Judaism. It might, accordingly, be expected that the new *ecclesia* would emphasize the distributive, as the old had expressed the comprehensive, idea. The actual partition of the unorganized Pentecostal community, erelong, into distinct churches widely scattered, the localization of the Epistles in title and contents, and the steady drift of apostolic usage, all confirm the impression that our Lord meant, from the beginning, to work out his purpose on earth especially through the agency of the local church, upon which he thereby put peculiar honor and abiding emphasis.

8. *Recapitulation.* It may be well, at this point, to pause and summarize briefly the chief results of our inquiry.

(1) We have found a recent increasing tendency among scholars to repudiate the notion, uniformly assented to "since the days of Augustine," that "church" and "kingdom" are identical. Dr. Candlish cites a long list of authorities to this effect. We may add also the influential names of Dr. Hort (previously referred to), James Orr and A. M. Fairbairn. Dr. Fairbairn (in his "Studies in the Life of Christ") has discussed the question in detail, pointing out the irreconcilable features of the two, and concluding that "the church and the kingdom may thus be more properly contrasted than compared." "The church was to pro-

mote the ends, realize the ideals of the kingdom. If *basileia* was steeped in Hebrew, *ecclesia* was penetrated with Greek associations." (Note the bearing of this last statement, in connection with what has been here urged.)

(2) The theory of identity, thus boldly abandoned after centuries of unhesitating acceptance, proves upon examination to have been uniformly and logically interlocked with the notion of a "church universal"; which still prevails, although confusedly interpreted. Both notions build upon the same Judæo-Christian hypothesis, and justify themselves by the same exegetic methods; both lend themselves to the support of the same type of ecclesiastical organization; and both seem to have had a common historic origin. For the "days of Augustine," to which we are referred for the beginning of the now exploded theory of identity, followed soon after the first "ecumenical" council and the established conception of an imperial church—the incipient stage of the later "Holy Roman Empire." From that time the imperial, the national, or the hereditary, theory of the church has been in the ascendant, and the exegetical pressure of

THE CHURCH OF THE NEW TESTAMENT

each has been in the same direction. Advancing scholarship has now overthrown one of these twin-born and indissolubly associated ideas. It can not be presumptuous to suspect that, under a like test, the other is doomed to the same fate. Truth is not ultimately settled by the voice of the majority, nor even by that of still unanimous tradition.

(3) Applying the ordinary principles of criticism to the text of the New Testament, we find a strong presumption in favor of popular usage, rather than the Septuagint, as the primary source of authority in determining the meaning of the words in question. Both words are Greek; both had a definite and familiar sense; both were taken originally from the political sphere, and had a radically antithetic signification. *Basileia* had come to designate the world-wide Roman Empire exclusively: while *ecclesia* had come to refer to various forms of local assembly, the Jews applying it familiarly to the individual synagogue.

(4) Our Lord's use of the words in the Gospels confirms the expectation thus aroused. He uses the word *ecclesia* but twice. In one of these instances he points

unequivocally to a local assembly taken as a "representative" of a class (to borrow Dr. Hort's characterization). In the other, where the two words are brought into juxtaposition, interpretation in the same sense makes the whole passage not only more intelligible, but harmonizes better with the figurative and historic implications of the context. The word *basileia,* as elsewhere occurring in his utterances, is coupled with allusions quite unintelligible as applied to a synonymous *ecclesia,* but consistent enough if the two are treated as in their nature to be "contrasted rather than compared."

(5) Turning to the Acts and Epistles where writer and reader are predominantly Hellenes or Hellenized, the presumption of conformity to popular Gentile conception naturally increases in force. Jowett says of the Greeks that "the intensity of their inner life rendered it impossible for them to amalgamate great masses of men. Besides, the idea itself was repugnant to the Greek mind." It could hardly be presumed that an intelligent writer, addressing a Greek constituency, would inject into a familiar word a sense not only unfamiliar, but "repugnant," to his reader's methods of thought; expect-

ing him to fish out intuitively the idea meant to be conveyed.

We discover, on referring to the text, that our expectation is again justified by cumulative circumstances.

a. While *basileia* is uniformly treated as single and universal, never concrete, and usually future, in reference, *ecclesia* is, with relatively few exceptions, limited by its plural form or its specific application, to an individual, visible, existing body.

b. The figures commonly employed as descriptive of the *ecclesia* ("body," "temple," "household") are such as wholly lose significance when evaporated into generality of interpretation. Some of the Lutheran divines illustrate the absurdity into which one may be betrayed by attempting thus illegitimately to expand the figure to fit it to a theory. For they soberly maintained the ubiquity of Christ's fleshly body.

c. The functions uniformly allotted to the *ecclesia* become impracticable when attributed to the unknown elect, to a heterogeneous collection of unaffiliated local or provincial bodies, or to an unorganized multitude of individual disciples. The assumptions and exhortations of the bulk of the

Epistles would be meaningless and profitless if considered as addressed to such a motley company.

At this point we may appeal to modern criticism for confirmation of the impression thus far independently created by examination of the test. From them we learn that

d. The list of exceptional cases in which the universal sense has hitherto been confidently assumed to attach to the word *ecclesia* must be still further pruned down. There remain only Ephesians and Colossians to draw upon—Epistles which are avowedly addressed to a constituency peculiarly strong in Gentile association. Even there the figure of the "temple" can not be made to yield a universal reference; and the other figures are rendered equivocal as witnesses, by the circumstance that they have all been used elsewhere by the same writer, and, without exception, have been locally applied by him.

e. Progressive recension of the text has steadily favored the contrasted meaning of the two words: unity of the *basileia* and plurality of *ecclesia* more and more appearing in the new text.

f. Finally, the effort to derive the universal sense, even in the few passages that remain, from the text itself, by ordinary exegetical treatment of the language, has been abandoned. Dr. Hort's admission that it must be artificially attached to the word by argumentative inference amounts to the denial that any such meaning inheres in the word itself. How much is meant by the statement that the notion of universality thus introduced is to be taken in the "theological," as contrasted with the "historical," sense is not quite clear. The words naturally suggested an intended antithesis of the ideal with the actual. And this is the only logical issue of his argument. This may be made plain from his use of the figure of the "wife" (Eph. 5:22, 23); to which our attention has not yet been especially given. While admitting that the Apostle has elsewhere invariably given it a local or individual sense, he finds in it here a prospective reference to the "bride" of Rev. 21:2: which latter passage refers retrospectively to the relation of husband and wife between Jehovah and Israel as described by the prophets. As the Apocalyptic "bride" represents the whole number of the redeemed, it is inferred that the like figure must here have a like breadth

THE CHURCH AND THE KINGDOM

of reach. To interpret a practical letter to living men by the mystic symbolism of the Apocalypse is, at the best, a precarious kind of exegesis. It will be observed that the vision referred to by John looks on to a time when the "first heaven and the first earth are passed away." The "bride" is not described as "the church," but the "holy city": a "throne" being in its midst; an idea wholly incongruous with all representations of the earthly *ecclesia*. The whole symbolism, therefore, belongs to that heavenly region to which modern scholarship, as already shown, refers the "general assembly and church of the firstborn" of Heb. 12:23 (who are expressly there associated with the "heavenly Jerusalem"); and it accordingly lies outside of the subject under discussion. The utmost claim of affinity between the figure as used by Paul and by John, respectively, is that the bridal "church" of the one is a type of the bridal "city" of the other. But the "city" is an organized municipality whose citizens are actually gathered together. The local *ecclesia* normally typifies this, as a universal *ecclesia,* made up of "all the members of all the churches," scattered and unaffiliated, can not.

THE CHURCH OF THE NEW TESTAMENT

The critics having thus lent so large sanction and reinforcement to the tendencies suggested by independent inquiry, we need not hesitate to venture a little further in the direction whither they point, but refuse as yet to go. They have repudiated, in turn, every one of the definitions of the Church universal hitherto given: assuring us that it can not, according to any fair interpretation of New Testament language, be composed of local churches, of national churches, of a hereditary line, or of the elect. They have torn away a large part of the textual foundation on which the universal theory has hitherto rested in apparent security, and rudely shaken all the remainder. They have confirmed the impression that the antithesis, familiar to the Greek popular mind, between *basileia* and *ecclesia,* is recognized and reflected in the New Testament. The inference is irresistible, that if *basileia* there be universal, *ecclesia* can not be. That is to say, there is not only no such universal Church as has ordinarily been believed; there is no warrant in the New Testament for faith in any such Church at all, as a present "historic" reality.

The Scripture knows but one "kingdom,"

THE CHURCH AND THE KINGDOM

for the time being "within" and invisible: to become visible in God's good time; and, in that sense, yet future. Over against this it sets, steadily and consistently, the "church" as a present, local, individual, visible organization, capable of indefinite multiplication.

PART VI.
CONTEMPORARY SIGNIFICANCE

I.

IMPORTANCE OF DISTINCTION URGED

It may seem that the question under discussion is, after all, only one of those strivings "about words to no profit" against which Paul cautions Timothy. For we all agree in recognizing a certain kind of unity, created by community of discipleship: all believers are "made one through the blood of Christ" in some sense. There remains, then, only the question of the right name to apply to this unity. And what harm can come of calling it the "universal church," as well as the "universal kingdom"?

The objection is plausible but fallacious. False names are the most insidious of deceivers. "Errors of nomenclature are apt to avenge themselves by generating errors of idea," as Coleridge truly observes. And such errors are particularly dangerous when we are dealing with the language of revelation. "The words of the Lord are pure words: as silver tried in a furnace of earth, purified seven times." We can not suppose that our Lord, or his apostles under his guidance, selected loosely the terms which were to be of so large significance in directing the development of the new movement. We must recognize some force in the peculiar expression, "If a man love me, he will keep my *words*." If we can be certain what words he used, and the precise idea he intended to convey by them, it will be presumptuous and hazardous to substitute new names or intrude new meanings into the old. "He that reproveth God, let him answer it." It no doubt seemed innocent, at first, to call the Lord's table an "altar," and the presiding minister a "priest"; it might even be defended as a natural inference from the sacrificial allusions connected with the rite in the New Testament. But out of this seemingly insignificant departure from New Testament nomenclature, arose the whole hierarchical system. The "bishop" of the New Testament was the "pastor" of a local church. The name was afterward expanded so as to describe a diocesan ruler unknown to the apostolic churches, and when the pastor became a "priest," the bishop became logically a "high priest." It is thought ab-

CONTEMPORARY SIGNIFICANCE

surd to apply the New Testament designation "bishop" to a local pastor to-day, while the diocesan officer has become a "lord bishop," in direct violation of Christ's prohibition of "lordship." The Pope's claim to be Pontifex Maximus is the logical outcome of the reckless disregard of authoritative Scriptural precedent in the use of titles.

The evil does not end with the confusion of thought arising from doubleness of meaning in the word. The new meaning, having nestled amicably beside the old, under the brooding shelter of a common title, rarely fails to attempt a cuckoo-like monopoly of the place. All the world once agreed that baptism was immersion only. Clinic submergence first offered itself as a confessedly imperfect substitute; then pouring was hesitatingly admitted as sufficient; then sprinkling. Neither of these progressively dwindling forms of the rite was claimed to be normal, but permissible only in emergency: but, once admitted, they soon became lawfully equivalent, and, in the Westminster Confession, finally exclusive. The word "baptize" no longer suggests to the average pedobaptist the faintest hint of its New Testament meaning. It has become, as a late

THE CHURCH AND THE KINGDOM

Chinese version shrewdly put it, "the watering ceremony."

It can not, then, be a matter of indifference whether the notion of universality, visible or invisible, shall be allowed to attach itself to a term to which it does not legitimately belong in the usage of either the Apostles or the early Christian writers. If Christ and his appointed messengers cautiously preserved the distinction between "church" and "kingdom," uniformly treating the former as local and visible, and the latter as universal and invisible, nothing but harm can come from blurring the line of demarcation which they have set, and so confusing their teaching concerning each. The two ideas—that of a local organism on the one side, and that of a scattered and unaffiliated world-community on the other—are too incongruous to dwell harmoniously together under a common designation. To admit the idea of a Church universal, at all, is to make that *"the* church," and relatively to derogate from the importance of, and the honor due to, the local churches. We have seen that this secondary and "theological" has already asserted itself to be the true and primary meaning of the word.

CONTEMPORARY SIGNIFICANCE

Then, as every idea seeks to embody itself, he who regards himself as a member of the Church universal will naturally seek to adjust himself to the demands of the larger, as more important than the smaller, body to which he also belongs. John H. Newman, smitten with enthusiasm for the Church universal, which must from its very nature be one and historically continuous, went logically to Rome. Others, dreaming of a like church as essentially ideal in organization, have looked contemptuously on the "sects"; exhorting men to join a kind of "choir invisible," where denominationalism shall no longer hinder the communion of saints. Such sentimentalism is apt to degenerate into a Christianity as "invisible" as the vaporous constituency to which it fancies itself allied. He who loves the Church universal, while despising the church particular, is of no particular use to either. God "setteth the solitary in families." This is as true in the religious as in the social sphere, and "free love" is as disreputable and baneful in one as in the other.

It ought not to be easily forgotten that all historic efforts at reformation in Christian history have been expressed in the

THE CHURCH AND THE KINGDOM

assertion of the rights and functions of the local, against the dogmatism and tyranny of the general, body: and that this has grown out of a return to Scriptural teaching and precedent. The early hermits and monastic communities were asserters, however mistaken in ascetic ideal, of individualism and household independence, against the tyranny of the overshadowing imperial ecclesiasticism. The Waldenses, the Petrobrussians, and divers other "heretics" of the Middle Ages, were, as Milman significantly terms them, "Biblical Anti-Sacerdotalists," who denied the exclusive claims of the one historically continuous universal Church. One of the prime doctrines of Luther, the doctrine that turned reformation into revolt, was the assertion of the priesthood of all believers, and the legitimacy of a freshly originated and self-organized church. The first ecumenical council under Constantine had issued the first authoritative creed, and its acceptance had been penally enforced. The Church universal, that is to say, announced its arrival by the introduction of dogmatism and persecution. Luther asserted the right of the individual to read, judge and obey for himself, and to combine with others

CONTEMPORARY SIGNIFICANCE

in the voluntary establishment of a free local organization, regulated and officered by independent election and ordination. He repudiated persecution: "the hangman is no doctor of divinity." But he was caught in the tangle of embarrassing circumstance, and faltered in the thorough working out of his reformatory principles. The state church accordingly arose: dogmatism returned as despotic as ever: the "hangman" was summoned again to remove heresy by removing the heretic: and Lutheranism lapsed from its incipient local independence. It remained for the early "Anabaptists," seconded at a later date by the Brownists of England, to break away from the universal or national body that had usurped the name of "the church," and as "seceders," "nonconformists," or "separatists," to assert the primitive and indefeasible right of the independent local body to the long-withheld title.

II.

BEARING ON SOME TENDENCIES OF THE PRESENT TIME

Abundant suggestions arise in connection with the subject discussed, which it is needless to enumerate in detail, or even to do more than hint at the bearing of those mentioned. There is a growing disposition among theological writers:

1. To follow the bad example of German critics in treating the text of the New Testament as unreliable, and reconstructing the narrative, especially the words of our Lord, from a speculative standpoint. Even Dr. Thayer, in his Lexicon, ventures to improve on the report of Matthew (16: 18) by the insinuation that "perhaps the Evangelist employs *ten ecclesian*, although Christ may have said *ten basileian mou*." Of course, if the more radical "higher critics" are right, and the text of Scripture is the mere *flotsam* and *jetsam* of current legend, caught together and rafted down to us by irresponsi-

CONTEMPORARY SIGNIFICANCE

ble hands, all opinions or practices based upon the use of specific words, are left defenseless. But we "have not so learned Christ."

2. Closely allied to the habit mentioned is the fashionable tendency to repudiate the authority and importance of the specific doctrine conveyed, even where the language and its meaning are not doubted. Prof. G. B. Adams, of Yale, tells us, in his "Civilization During the Middle Ages," that "the Christian apostle did not demand belief in any system of intellectual truth. The primitive Christianity had apparently no required theology. He did not demand that certain rites and ceremonies should be performed." So that they were to believe without drawing on the intellect, to accept Christ as the Son of God without dabbling in theology, and to be baptized without submitting to any rite!

3. Another feature of current theological speculation is the manifestation of a decided drift toward Universalism. It reveals itself in many ways. New emphasis upon the incarnation of Christ, as of itself either revealing or effecting redemption, wholly apart from his atoning death, is one of its forms of expression. Its catch-words are becoming

familiar: such, for instance, as "the fatherhood of God and the brotherhood of man," as the essence of the gospel; or the "solidarity of humanity," as involving necessarily the corporate salvation of the race. Canon Fremantle, in his "World as the Subject of Redemption," plainly says that Paul, in Ephesians 1, speaks of the whole human race, which, he declares, "was chosen in Christ before the foundation of the world to be the adopted children of God. . . . The purpose of God is absolutely universal." All men, he further says, are undergoing "unconscious and proleptic" processes of regeneration: they "absorb" Christianity from their "environment." There is thus a "substratum of truth" in baptismal regeneration; which, in the case of infants, is an expression of the fact that the "house" as well as the intelligent believer at its head is being saved. The picturesque illustration of this supposed religious brotherhood of the race was a prominent purpose of the famous "World's Parliament of Religions" at Chicago. "In the center," according to the account of an enthusiastic participator, "clad in scarlet robes, and seated in a high chair of state, was Cardinal Gibbons, the

CONTEMPORARY SIGNIFICANCE

highest prelate of his church in the United States, who, as was fitting in this Columbian year, was to open the meeting with prayer. On either side of him were grouped the Oriental delegates, w h o s e many-colored raiment vied with his own in brilliancy. Conspicuous among these followers of Brahma and Buddha and Mohammed was the eloquent monk Vivekananda of Bombay, clad in gorgeous red apparel," etc. The Lord's Prayer was used by the assembly under the leadership of a Jewish Rabbi, and the benediction of the "eight million deities of Japan" invoked upon those present by a Shinto priest. Thus Christianity took its place as one of the many allied phases of the "absolute religion" in the "universal church" of humanity.

4. Closely associated, and m a r c h i n g easily in line with these conceptions, is that of Christianity as the product of, and destined to reach its completion through, the agency of natural "evolution." The "New Jerusalem," Canon Fremantle assures us, is "not a heavenly state beyond this world," but "a progressively righteous state in this world." Nor is it to be a "society of worship and teaching," for there is to be "no

temple therein." A specious justification of this conception of Christianity as mastering the world by subtle diffusion, without intervening organism or doctrine, is sought in the parable of the leaven; through whose silent permeation the "whole" world is to be "leavened." This figure, it is said, precisely describes the process, and foretells the result, of the steady ripening and broadening of Christian sentiment and the pioneering invasion of outlying nations by Christian culture and civilization. Thus, by purely natural processes, the world is developing into the "kingdom of heaven." Such interpreters are usually conveniently content with this one only of all the "parables of the kingdom": they are careful not to molest, or let themselves be molested by, the fate of the tares or of the bad fish caught in the net. Those who contend for a *"scientific evolution"* of Christianity seem ordinarily to "understand neither what they say nor whereof they affirm." The evolution they conceive of is not scientific, and the Christianity they would unfold is not Christian. Science can not recognize the supernatural as a factor in its researches; and Christianity is empty of significance without it. To

CONTEMPORARY SIGNIFICANCE

surrender the incarnation of Deity in Christ, his miracles, his resurrection, the immediate work of the Holy Spirit in man, regeneration, revelation, is to leave an empty husk. But no scientist would claim these as within the range of the natural.

It is obvious that the four vagaries, thus alluded to, start from, and are largely governed by, a common conception. Beginning with the idea of the "kingdom of heaven" as invisible, unorganized, and destined to become universal, and reckoning the "church" as only another name for the same thing, Christianity has been reduced in conception to a kind of atmosphere of sentiment; a vague effluence too ethereal to be formulated into a doctrinal form, or to find concrete expression in a visible organization. Such a Christianity is apt to content itself with the current revelations of the "Christian consciousness" in lieu of the written Word; with the "Christ of to-day"—that is, the ideal Christ—in exchange for the historic person of the Gospel narrative, and with an "immanent" God, scarcely, if at all, distinguishable from the "resident forces" of the physical universe, as a substitute for the living God of Scripture. Of course the individual

THE CHURCH AND THE KINGDOM

church becomes not simply superfluous, but positively obstructive, in such a scheme.

But, aside from these theoretic rhapsodies, there are some movements of a practical character, within and without the churches, which suggest a similar source and drift. Among these we may observe

5. Growing laxity with reference to Christ's ordinances. The Lord's Supper was instituted in connection with the Passover, which was a household ordinance: "No stranger may eat of it." It was from the beginning the center and characteristic expression of the fraternal life of the single church. When the episcopate had crept in, the diocese in due time became the "church." Then the bishop, consecrating the elements in the "cathedral" center, distributed them to the local "parts" of the body. When there came to be a world-bishop, all the members of the one ecumenical church might communicate anywhere in any part thereof lawfully. So came "open communion." Of late denominational assemblies and conglomerate religious bodies of the most heterogeneous composition have spread the household table in the market-place, so to speak. And in many churches the door of admission to the

CONTEMPORARY SIGNIFICANCE

local table is thrown open to those who belong to the "universal church," or think they do, without either baptism or profession of faith in Christ in any form.

6. A noteworthy phenomenon of the times is the rapid multiplication of newly invented schemes for the prosecution of work alleged either to have been left undone by, or not to be within the province of, the individual church. "Societies," "leagues," "alliances," and the like, have sprung up in swift succession, each aspiring to a worldwide sway in some particular field of activity. It is, perhaps, too early to pronounce upon the net results of some of these movements; and they have been inaugurated by men too far above suspicion of unworthy motives to justify harsh criticism. But sincerity of purpose, or even temporary fruitfulness of good, should not exempt any novelty from cautious inquiry as to its natural tendencies. If our Lord intended the local church to be the normal object of personal affection and field of personal activity, we must look with jealousy upon any actual rival, whether or not rivalry be admitted or disavowed. The question naturally arises whether under the law of gravi-

tation, which holds alike in the social as in the physical world, a body revolving loyally around a smaller center can come within the sweep of a larger, and not be disturbed in its proper orbit. Will the local attachment and steady efficiency of the individual disciple be best promoted by dependence for freshened enthusiasm upon the feverish impulse of an occasional monster meeting, and by looking for spiritual guidance to official utterances from a remote organic center? Will the absorption into a common treasury, of funds enough to defray the expenses of great assemblies, national or international; the establishment of a costly newspaper organ; the payment of salaries and of sending its officials round the world—in nowise deplete the resources of affiliated churches, or divert them from more aggressive forms of Christian work? It is possible that good may, on the whole, result: it is certain that a tremendous kind of agency for good or ill here awaits the test of time.

7. "Christian socialism" may be referred to in this connection. Professor Herron and his colleagues never weary in denouncing the "institutional church" as utterly failing to comprehend its mission. The "kingdom

CONTEMPORARY SIGNIFICANCE

of heaven" is, according to their theory, not to be brought in by the sentimental process of "saving souls," but by improving tenement-houses and revolutionizing our social arrangements.

They agree substantially with Canon Fremantle, that "the prayer 'Thy will be done' leads directly into politics." The business of Christians, according to the learned Canon, is "to make the kingdoms of this world into kingdoms not of this world." Save the ship, and the passengers will be thereby saved. When the "kingdom of England" has, through wise legislation, been transformed into a local "kingdom of heaven," the "worshiping church" will have completed its provisional work and become effete. "Civilization has now reached a point at which the eyes of all Christian men should be turned distinctly in the direction of the universal church, with a view to its organization" (by turning all civil governments into a confederate "kingdom of heaven.") How simple and feasible—especially in view of the present millennial attitude of these inchoate "kingdoms of heaven"! From the days of John the Baptist men have been seeking to bring in the Kingdom of heaven by violence. They have been determined to hasten the growing mustard-tree by heaving at its roots. And too often they have listened to Satan's temptation, which Christ refused; hastening to set up the Devil's kingdom in Christ's name, or to "weed the garden of the Lord with Satan's borrowed dibble."

8. The same passion for consolidation which has produced "trusts" in finance, and "imperialism" in politics, seems to have infected the Christian realm. The worship of ancient Pan has revived. We have had pan-Presbyterian, pan-Congregational, and other ecumenical assemblies, as before noted; to say nothing of the "World's Parliament of Religions," which, in view of its large representation of the heathen gods, might aptly have been called pandemonium. It has been soberly proposed, according to the newspapers, to organize a "religious trust" in Maine, to prevent sectarian squandering in the establishment of churches. For denominationalism has been widely denounced as the chief hindrance to the more rapid advance of Christianity at home and abroad. It seems to be forgotten that this first denominational century is the great century

CONTEMPORARY SIGNIFICANCE

of missionary conquest. Such competent observers as Philip Schaff and Theodore Christlieb assure us that the coincidence is logical and not casual.

The sermon on "The Talisman of Unity," before mentioned, was preached in the new five-million-dollar cathedral now building for the "Bishop of New York" (where the rival Roman Catholic claimant of the same title already has his "throne" in like imposing structure, flanked by a gorgeous marble "palace" for his private occupancy). The new cathedral, located in an aristocratic section of the city, is designed, as has been explained, to show to the whole population, by its massiveness and splendor, how great and beneficent a thing Christianity is. Meanwhile "local churches" among the starving and bemired population of the "submerged" districts have, one by one, "folded their tents, like the Arabs, and silently stolen away," because of lack of financial resources.

The sermon referred to, preached in the crypt beneath the apse of the great building, refers to the "chapels of the tongues" which are to radiate from the apse above, as symbolic of its cosmopolitan function and purpose. Mere unity of sentiment, the preacher

THE CHURCH AND THE KINGDOM

argues, is an "iridescent dream," if taken as the realization of the "universal church." That must be an actuality, with a real organization and a real nucleus of control. What better than the "Apostles' Creed" and the "Historic Episcopate"? for the Episcopal Church shelters happily under her wing the Romanizing ritualist and the intolerant Puritan.

Professor Shields (who afterward gravitated from the Presbyterian to the Episcopal body) hoped for a consolidation of Christendom which would take in "those Unitarian churches which express the flower of Puritan culture, as well as the great Roman Catholic Church, which is already in the lead on such social questions as marriage, temperance, education and property." The "iridescent dream" of a universal Church will, then, when realized, take in one group which refuses to exclude from its pulpits those who "can not conscientiously believe in God," and another who worship a piece of bread!

The often urged notion that a "united front" of Protestantism against Romanism, or of Christianity against heathenism, will be irresistible, is itself a relic of heathen-

CONTEMPORARY SIGNIFICANCE

ism. It is the old "trusting in horses and chariots," which the Scripture condemns. No massing of inherent weakness can bring strength. "Not by might, nor by power, but by my Spirit, saith the Lord."

III.

PRACTICAL CONCLUSIONS

Finally, we may set down the following practical conclusions. The "kingdom of heaven" as an organized *regime* will come in due time; but its introduction is God's affair, not ours. He will "hasten it in his time." The New Jerusalem, when it appears, is not to be built after human device, nor built from below by human hands: it will "descend out of heaven from God."

Meantime, the "kingdom of heaven" now exists in the earth only as a "kingdom within." We can enter it only as it enters us, through individual regeneration. As it has pleased God to inaugurate his Kingdom through the individual man, so has it equally pleased him to develop and propagate it through the church, which is also individual. Into a Christian household every new-born soul should normally be born: to it his affection and allegiance are primarily due: in it he is to be molded and equipped for

CONTEMPORARY SIGNIFICANCE

service: and from it he is to go forth to help men heavenward. Here is the only earthly agency divinely appointed for the development of Christian character and the propagation of Christian faith. Here let men be content to be "fellow-workers unto the kingdom of God." No human devices can compel that Kingdom "immediately to appear." The "universal church invisible," if there were one, could offer us no specific place for service, since it must remain ideal only. Let every man "abide in the calling wherein he is called," doing "with his might what his hand finds to do," and he will be sure to do the best thing, because the thing which God has appointed. The best medium for the fulfillment of God's plans is that which God himself has chosen.

There is no record of a "gospel of the church," but only of a "gospel of the kingdom"—a kingdom to be "manifested" in due time. Meantime the "manifold wisdom of God" is *"now"* to be "made known through *the church"* (Eph. 4: 10). Let him who would hasten the coming of the end not pervert or despise the appointed means.

THE END.

A BIOGRAPHICAL SKETCH OF JESSE BURGESS THOMAS (1832-1915)

BY

JOHN FRANKLIN JONES

A
Biographical Sketch
of
Jesse Burgess Thomas
(1832-1915)

Jesse Burgess Thomas was born July 29, 1832 at Edwardsville, Illinois. He was the son of Jesse B. Thomas, Illinois Supreme Court judge (Cathcart) and Adeline Clarissa (Smith) Thomas. Several members of the family were distinguished members of the legal profession (*DAB*).

He graduated Kenyon College, Ohio, in 1850 and was admitted to the Illinois bar in 1855 (1852, [*DAB*]). He entered Rochester Theological Seminary in 1852 to prepare for ministry, but ill health necessitated his leaving after a short period. He pursued the mercantile business in Chicago for a time (Cathcart).

He was ordained a Baptist minister in 1862. He served as pastor at Waukegan, Illinois (1862-64), the Pierrepont Street church, Brooklyn, New York (1864-68); the First Baptist Church, San Francisco, California (1868-69); the Michigan Avenue church, Chicago, Illinois (1869-1874), and the First Baptist Church, Brooklyn, New York (1874) ("Thomas"). The church's edifice burned and it united services with the Pierpont Street church and the two eventually united as one church (Cathcart).

In 1887 he became a professor of church history (*DAB*) in the theological seminary located at Newton Centre, Massachusetts. He received the D.D. degree from the University of Chicago in 1866. He authored *The Old Bible and the New Science* (New York, 1877) ("Thomas"); "Significance of the Historic Element in Scripture," in Joseph Cook's *Christ and Modern Thought* (1881) (*DAB*); and *The Mould of Doctrine* (Philadelphia, 1883) ("Thomas"); *Some Parables of Nature* (1911); and *The Church and the Kingdom, a New Testament Study* (1914) (*DAB*).

Thomas was an orator, first-rate scholar, dramatic in preaching style, persuasive, and impassioned. His lectures on the theories of modern skeptics are equal, if not superior, to those of Joseph Parker (Cathcart).

He married Abbie Anne Eastman of Ottawa County, Michigan May 30, 1855. The couple have five sons and three daughters; four children died young. Thomas died June 6, 1915 in Brooklyn, New York (*DAB*).

BIBLIOGRAPHY

Cathcart, William, ed. *The Baptist Encyclopaedia: A Dictionary of the Doctrines, Ordinances, Usages, Confessions of Faith, Sufferings, Labors, and Successes, and of the General History of the Baptist Denomination in All Lands, with Numerous Biographical Sketches of Distinguished American and Foreign Baptist, and a Supplement*. Philadelphia, Louis H. Everts, 1881; reprint, Paris, AR: Baptist Standard Bearer, 1988. S.v. "Thomas, Jesse B., D.D."

Dumas, Malone, ed. *Dictionary of American Biography* (1864 edition). S.v."Thomas, Jesse Burgess."

"Jesse Burgess Thomas." Article on-line. Available at http://www.famousamericans.net/ jesseburgessthomas/. Accessed July 6, 2004.

BY JOHN FRANKLIN JONES
CORDOVA, TENNESSEE
JULY 2004

THE BAPTIST STANDARD BEARER, INC.

a non-profit, tax-exempt corporation
committed to the Publication & Preservation
of the Baptist Heritage.

CURRENT TITLES AVAILABLE IN
THE BAPTIST *DISTINCTIVES* SERIES

KIFFIN, WILLIAM	A Sober Discourse of Right to Church-Communion. Wherein is proved by Scripture, the Example of the Primitive Times, and the Practice of All that have Professed the Christian Religion: That no Unbaptized person may be Regularly admitted to the Lord's Supper. (London: George Larkin, 1681).
KINGHORN, JOSEPH	Baptism, A Term of Communion. (Norwich: Bacon, Kinnebrook, and Co., 1816)
KINGHORN, JOSEPH	A Defense of "Baptism, A Term of Communion". In Answer To Robert Hall's Reply. (Norwich: Wilkin and Youngman, 1820).
GILL, JOHN	Gospel Baptism. A Collection of Sermons, Tracts, etc., on Scriptural Authority, the Nature of the New Testament Church and the Ordinance of Baptism by John Gill. (Paris, AR: The Baptist Standard Bearer, Inc., 2006).

CARSON, ALEXANDER	Ecclesiastical Polity of the New Testament. (Dublin: William Carson, 1856).
BOOTH, ABRAHAM	A Defense of the Baptists. A Declaration and Vindication of Three Historically Distinctive Baptist Principles. Compiled and Set Forth in the Republication of Three Books. Revised edition. (Paris, AR: The Baptist Standard Bearer, Inc., 2006).
BOOTH, ABRAHAM	Paedobaptism Examined on the Principles, Concessions, and Reasonings of the Most Learned Paedobaptists. With Replies to the Arguments and Objections of Dr. Williams and Mr. Peter Edwards. 3 volumes. (London: Ebenezer Palmer, 1829).
CARROLL, B. H.	*Ecclesia* - The Church. With an Appendix. (Louisville: Baptist Book Concern, 1903).
CHRISTIAN, JOHN T.	Immersion, The Act of Christian Baptism. (Louisville: Baptist Book Concern, 1891).
FROST, J. M.	Pedobaptism: Is It From Heaven Or Of Men? (Philadelphia: American Baptist Publication Society, 1875).
FULLER, RICHARD	Baptism, and the Terms of Communion; An Argument. (Charleston, SC: Southern Baptist Publication Society, 1854).
GRAVES, J. R.	Tri-Lemma: or, Death By Three Horns. The Presbyterian General Assembly Not Able To Decide This Question: "Is Baptism In The Romish Church Valid?" 1st Edition.

	(Nashville: Southwestern Publishing House, 1861).
MELL, P.H.	Baptism In Its Mode and Subjects. (Charleston, SC: Southern Baptist Publications Society, 1853).
JETER, JEREMIAH B.	Baptist Principles Reset. Consisting of Articles on Distinctive Baptist Principles by Various Authors. With an Appendix. (Richmond: The Religious Herald Co., 1902).
PENDLETON, J.M.	Distinctive Principles of Baptists. (Philadelphia: American Baptist Publication Society, 1882).
THOMAS, JESSE B.	The Church and the Kingdom. A New Testament Study. (Louisville: Baptist Book Concern, 1914).
WALLER, JOHN L.	Open Communion Shown to be Unscriptural & Deleterious. With an introductory essay by Dr. D. R. Campbell and an Appendix. (Louisville: Baptist Book Concern, 1859).

For a complete list of current authors/titles, visit our internet site at:
www.standardbearer.org
or write us at:

he Baptist Standard Bearer, Inc.

NUMBER ONE IRON OAKS DRIVE • PARIS, ARKANSAS 72855
TEL # 479-963-3831　　　　　　　　FAX # 479-963-8083
EMAIL: Baptist@centurytel.net　　http://www.standardbearer.org

Thou hast given a standard to them that fear thee; that it may be displayed because of the truth. — Psalm 60:4

www.ingramcontent.com/pod-product-compliance
Lightning Source LLC
Chambersburg PA
CBHW021754230426
43669CB00006B/74